ENCOUNTERS
with
God

The Story of A Man's
Personal Encounters with God

Joe Centineo

Cover art by Scott Burks

BurkhartBooks
www.burkhartbooks.com
Bedford, Texas

Dedication

I dedicate this book to my Lord and Savior Jesus Christ. His life, death and resurrection are the basis by which we can have "Encounters With God."

Acknowledgments

Many friends and church members have encouraged me to record my journey with God in book form so that others may be encouraged in their personal journeys to recognize God in the daily events of their lives. I want to recognize the contributions of several people who have been instrumental in bringing Encounters with God to fruition.

Thanks to Greg Mulkey for encouraging me to put my encounters with God in writing. Also, thanks to Debi Moore for her many hours of writing. Without her help, this book would never have happened. Ann Hedgepeth, thank you for your work transcribing my sermons. Thanks to Caroline Watson, whose skills in grammar were instrumental in the writing of this book. Special thanks to Valerie Parenica, Steve Moore, and especially to my sister, Chris Centineo, who spent many hours editing this book.

I would like to thank my children, who have been such a blessing to me through all of our trials and our good times. And, thanks to my wife, Toni, my friend and partner through life and through all the lessons God has taught me.

Most importantly, I give thanks to my Lord and Savior Jesus Christ, who saved me from the pit of despair and gave me life and purpose. He has never stopped patiently teaching me the lessons He has for me to learn.

Joe Centineo

Contents

Ministering God's Way

The School of Brokenness - Part I

The School of Brokenness - Part 2

Preface

The greatest thing that happened in my life was finding God through Jesus Christ. God has had His hand on me since I met Him, and to my delight, He has interacted with me on numerous occasions in very personal ways. At times, He has spoken to me—not in an audible voice, but softly, in ways that I cannot attribute to anyone or anything else. At other times I have recognized God leading me through the words of other people. I have learned many lessons on my journey with God: many learned the hard way; others learned with a sense of humor. I believe there is value in sharing our journeys with other people.

This book is a series of events that God has used to teach me to trust Him and His path for my life. Its focus is the amazing, awesome God of the universe and how He has interacted with me and guided my life. From the moment that I let Jesus Christ into my heart, everything began to change. Even to this day, Jesus continues to change and to guide me.

I pray that this book will encourage you to see the hand of God at work in your own life. We are told in Jeremiah 29:13 that when we seek after God with all of our heart, we will find Him. I have found that to be true in my life. He offers you the same type of guidance. It is my prayer that in reading this book, you will be encouraged to seek God's direction for your life.

Blessings to you as you journey with God.

Joe Centineo

2014

Introduction

My Life Before Christ

Shortly after I was born in Brooklyn, New York, my family had to move because my dad did something that offended some of the Italian mobsters in our neighborhood. It involved a lot of money so we moved to Long Island to hide out until things quieted down. Once the situation calmed, we were able to move back to the East Flatbush section of Brooklyn where I spent the majority of my younger years.

Like most kids growing up in Brooklyn, I fell in love with baseball and the Yankees, then football and the New York Giants. I played a lot of sandlot sports. No organized teams, just a bunch of neighborhood kids getting together in a city park playing football or baseball, trying not to break any car windows or get hurt being tackled on the harsh asphalt. We played from early morning until the sun set, with only a short break when our moms called us in for dinner. I had a normal Brooklyn childhood—if a Brooklyn childhood could be called normal. But, as I approached my teen years, a not-so-normal involvement with drugs, alcohol, and violence enveloped me.

Brooklyn in the early '70s was a place where kids raised themselves and morality was determined by the rules of the street. I remember wanting to do the right thing but never really knowing what the right thing was. As Italian Catholics, my family occasionally went to church on Sundays, but it had little effect on me. My parents seemed to think it was important for me to be a "good boy," but they had very little influence on my behavior. I played by the rules of the street.

To my friends on the streets, power and respect were determined by strength and toughness. Being the top dog in the neighborhood was a coveted position, and that top person had to do whatever it took to keep his place there.

My older brother Bob understood this. He used my tenacity and fighting ability to earn our way to the top. I was a small, undersized brawler, the small kid you'd bet against in a street fight. My brother counted on people's initial impressions of me to make a lot of money. Though I was small, I could beat up almost anyone in the neighborhood. I was fast and tough.

We made money fighting. Bob and I would visit a neighborhood and arrange for me to fight a small kid, one just a little bigger than me. I would win that fight, and then the other kids would line up to take shots at me. The outcome was always the same. Bob and I would go home richer, and I became the "top dog" of the neighborhood.

Although I should have been riding high because of my victories, I usually felt bad inside. I wouldn't admit it, but I didn't enjoy fighting, and I didn't like hurting other kids. But…it was what I was good at. If I had stopped fighting,

I would have lost any feelings I had of self-worth or personal value. I earned a lot of respect and street credibility, but not much inner peace.

I seemed like a normal kid in those days. The chaos that existed inside me was well hidden. No one suspected that by the time I reached Junior High I was already drinking alcohol and smoking pot three times a day. Most kids my age couldn't drink a quart of gin, but I was able to. It landed me in the hospital, but it was the price I paid for being "cool."

When I began to date, I noticed that my street values didn't lend themselves to any moral boundaries. I treated girls as a commodity. I did not respect them, their feelings, or their bodies. Street values also contributed to my committing several crimes: stealing parking meters, stealing cars, and breaking into warehouses. Eventually, I was arrested. I allowed the wrong people to influence me, and I made wrong decisions. I didn't blame the other kids; I had committed the crimes. I wanted to do the right thing, but I didn't know any other way other than the ways of the street.

When I reached high school, football and baseball were extremely important to me. I was a good athlete, but smoking pot negatively affected my ability to play. I knew I couldn't continue to do drugs and still achieve my goals on the playing field. This became clear to me the time I got high the night before a JV football game. During the first half of the game I was still high. Then an opponent hit me so hard that it knocked me straight. I learned that I couldn't be my best at sports if I messed with drugs.

I cleaned myself up and had a great high school sports career. I played three years as a running back on the football team and centerfielder on the baseball team. I made the local papers with a few game-winning performances in football and had good success on the baseball field. Sports were my love, and I intended to play in college and hopefully beyond.

My father didn't want me to go to college to play sports. He wanted me to work in a landscaping business he was buying for me and my brother so he offered me a bribe. If I stayed home to work in the landscaping business he would buy me any brand-new car that I chose. My love of material things won, and I chose the car over college sports. I have regretted that decision ever since. My choice to go into the landscaping business taught me to work hard and to earn a living. But it didn't keep me from making many of the wrong choices I had made in the past.

While in the landscaping business I'd work hard all week and then go out to the discos and get drunk on the weekends. At the discos, I had one goal: hook up with the prettiest girl in the club. That was my life.

Deep down, I wasn't happy. I was part owner of a thriving landscaping business with money to burn. I was on my second new car and had my own apartment. But I knew these things would never give me fulfillment. There had to be more to life, but I sure didn't know what it was. So I settled for what I had, thinking that even if it wasn't all I wanted, it would have to be enough.

Then I met an amazing girl and I was swept away. She was beautiful; we got along great; and I fell in love. We moved in together, and she became the center of my life. We often talked and planned for what life would be like if we were married. I banked my future on the expectation that she was the girl I was going to marry.

Everything seemed to be going my way until one day my world was blown apart. One of my friends pulled me aside and told me that my girlfriend had been cheating on me for the past two years—even while we lived together. He and some of my other friends knew about it. I seemed to be the only one who didn't know. My friends had kept quiet because they didn't want me to get hurt, but that night, one of my friends decided that he needed to tell me what had been going on.

My friend dropped that bomb and my world stopped spinning. I felt as if I had hit the ground so hard that the life was knocked out of me. My girlfriend's betrayal cut me deeply. I was humiliated and hurt, so I reverted to the street values I held as a kid. I began thinking in irrational, violent terms. I considered killing myself. At least that would stop the pain I felt. Then I thought about killing her. I was ashamed of having such a horrible thought, but it somehow seemed an appropriate punishment for what she had done. The pain she put me through caused me to seriously consider those two horrible choices.

I found myself at a crossroad. The real possibility that I could kill myself or kill someone else sickened me. I realized I had hit bottom. I wasn't sure if I really wanted to make it to tomorrow. I was in a place of such darkness that I was not sure I could recover. At the very least, I would never be the same again. I felt trapped between two evils with no way of escape. Neither was a choice I wanted to make, but I was so shattered. What was I to do?

It was then that I cried out to God and He touched my heart. I can't explain it any better than that. He reached into my shattered, quivering heart and touched it. I knew then that God was real. I had been lost in a terrible darkness, but He found me and showed me the way out. I wanted to seek out this God and discover who He was. I wanted to thank Him.

The next Sunday, I was invited to attend a church in Staten Island called Gateway Cathedral. I attended hoping to find God. I observed the people in this church who seemed to have a joy and happiness that I had never experienced. For the next three weeks I attended that church without really listening to the pastor's sermon. I watched the people. I was beginning to think that they had "something" that was missing in my own life. On the fourth Sunday that I attended the church, I finally listened to the pastor's sermon. He preached about Jesus Christ dying for our sins so we could be forgiven. I realized that I needed Christ to be my personal Savior. I responded to the pastor's invitation and put my faith and trust in Jesus Christ.

That began a relationship with God through Jesu
It was the most important decision I have ever m
    The remainder of this book chronicles my re
with this amazing God, and how He teaches me to listen
and to obey. I hope you will be encouraged and inspired by
my story. I also hope you will pursue a relationship with
God through Jesus Christ and begin your own story of
your personal walk with God.

The School of Discipleship

Chapter One

Starting Out

When the movie *Saturday Night Fever* hit the big screen in the 70's, it swept the nation influencing the younger generation with its exciting portrayal of night life. John Travolta, its star, was Disco King and the icon of my world. Every guy from my Brooklyn neighborhood—including me—aspired to be John Travolta. I purchased a replica of Travolta's white suit from the same store on King's Highway that had outfitted the movie. I lived in the 70's disco scene—the friends, the girls, the excitement of the dance floor—but its shallowness soon caused me to stumble toward emptiness. I knew I wanted something more.

I was twenty-two when I became a Christian and entered a church world that was totally different from my world of discos and exciting night life. When I gave my life to Christ, I gladly let go of the world that had been so familiar yet left me disillusioned and disappointed. To my delight, I knew in my heart that God had something special for me—a calling, a new way of living. I didn't know exactly what it was, but I sensed a destiny—something that God had for me to do. The thought that the Creator of the Universe wanted to use me, a young man with a mistake-filled past, inspired me to do anything and every-thing that the Lord asked me to do. I was so grateful that I was no longer lost.

Looking back on those early years, I recognize that I wasn't ready for the great adventure just yet. God had to spend some years focusing on the development of my character before the adventure could begin. God wanted me to become a man of faithfulness; a man that would be worthy of His trust. To make me into that man, God had to free me from some wrong thinking and wrong habits I had developed. He had to help me become a man of godly character. There began the process of transforming me into a disciple of Christ.

God chose to do much of my early character develop-ment at the church on Staten Island where I had surren-dered my life to Him. I became deeply involved in this church. I lived in Brooklyn at the time—a forty-five minute drive to the church. I often drove there five times a week. I didn't care that it was a long drive; I wanted to discover what God had in store for me. I listened, and I learned sitting in the comfortable seats of that wonderful church.

One of the first verses I memorized as a new Christian was John 14:21:

Whoever has My commands and obeys them, he is the one who loves Me.

Knowing about obedience and being obedient are two different things. As Ruler, Lord, and King, God has the right to expect our obedience in every aspect of our lives, even when it is difficult. God wants us to develop a life-style of obedience.

Over the next couple of years it became obvious to me that God was teaching me obedience. He led me through a series of tests to see if I was willing to commit my life to choosing God's way rather than my way. I was tested in areas both large and small to help me understand what God wanted of me. I began to understand what He expected, and I did my best to obey Him.

The first area in which God tested my obedience was in the arena of friendships.

I know people make fun of discos and disco music today, but back in my day the music and the club scene were king. The excitement of the disco made it seem like it was the place to be and most people—dressed to kill—frequented these places in an attempt to be a part of the cool crowd. Yet, behind the lights and excitement lurked darkness and emptiness. At their core, the clubs were merely well-packaged meat markets. For a guy, the object of the night was to fulfill one goal: possess the pretty girl. Guys were rarely interested in a girl as a person. It was as if they were looking in a butcher's window for the perfect slab of meat to take home and consume. That's what my friends and I did when we went clubbing. We would drive for an hour or so to get to a great disco and then spend a few hours there. We only stayed long enough to meet a pretty girl, and then we were gone. We weren't into anything long-term with these girls—no one seemed to be. Everyone knew the rules of the game and those who were part of it didn't try to buck the system. We were playing a dangerous game with painful consequences.

When I came to Christ, I didn't do an instant 180 degree turn. It took time for the Holy Spirit to lead me out of the mess that I had created in my life. Like many new Christians, I continued to follow along with the same crowd I had been hanging out with.

One night after having been a Christian for only a few weeks, I was out with six of my friends on the way to a club. I tried to tell them about Jesus. I know that was probably not the best time or place for a deep theological discussion, but I was so new at this Christianity business that I didn't understand that. I wanted to be with my friends so that I could have a positive impact on them. If that meant hanging out with them as usual on a Saturday night, then so be it.

Though my friends were on the prowl, I had changed. I didn't want to look lustfully at girls anymore. I was more interested in the souls of my friends. I tried to share Christ with them on the way to the club, but they kept changing the subject. However, I wouldn't quit. It must have gotten annoying because at one point they began to call me "Father Joe." I didn't take the hint and kept on plowing forward. I knew how wonderful it felt to know that Christ had forgiven me and set me free, and I wanted them to experience that forgiveness and freedom as well. Nevertheless, they were out for a good time and they didn't want to listen to me "preach."

Eventually, they got tired of hearing all of this "Jesus stuff" so they launched a two-pronged attack once we got to the club. Sadly, it was pretty successful. First, they began buying me drinks. My friends had rarely bought drinks for me before, but this night the alcohol was flowing and they were buying me round after round. They were hoping to get me drunk so I'd stop preaching to them. They succeeded. I drank too much.

Next, I was approached randomly by several women: all good-looking; all seeming to find me attractive and wanting to get to know me. I was thinking, "I am the man!" Though I am a decent-looking guy, I know I am no Brad Pitt! But you would never have known it that night. I was drawing them in like flies! I mean the girls were coming out of the woodwork! I never was able to confirm this, but I think my friends were paying the girls to hit on me. I guess they figured that as long as I was talking to someone else, I'd stop preaching to them. So, I talked with the girls and drank a little more, and…the plan worked. My buddies were left alone and ultimately had a good time without me.

It can be extremely hard to be a new Christian. We fall in love with the Lord, but our friends don't quite get what has happened to us. We continue to hang out with our old friends, but they can't seem to understand the change that's come over us. They misinterpret our concern for them as being "preachy" or judgmental of their lifestyle.

That's how things were going for me regarding my circle of friends. I went out to clubs on weekend nights with my old friends hoping to influence them for Christ. But in the end, they were the ones who were influencing me. I'd go home groggy and guilty from the experience and then have to struggle to get up the next morning to go to church. Once at church and exhausted from the happenings of the night before, I would struggle to stay awake. And then the guilt would come. I knew better. I knew I shouldn't have been in church with a hangover, but honestly, these were not only my closest friends, they were my only friends. Though they were my only option for a social life, I realized that I needed to put some distance between us and to develop more Christ-centered relationships.

One Saturday night my cousin Rick called and asked if I wanted to go clubbing with some of the guys. Normally, I would have gone, but the club scene was growing old for me. I was also getting a little depressed over my limited social options as a young Christian. Bored with the pace of the weekend, I was about to give in and go clubbing when I heard a little voice whisper, "Don't go."

I had heard that faint voice before, and I wondered if it might be God. I gave a non-committal answer to my cousin, hung up the phone and asked, "God? Was that You?" He didn't answer. I was torn between what I wanted to do and what I thought I should do. I needed another opinion to break the tie. I thought that my Mom might be able to help. She had a quiet sense of elegance and dignity that could always still the chaos of my world. However, I knew that she would not be able to help me this time. Although I loved my mom dearly and knew that she loved me, she wasn't yet a Christian. It was too much to expect her to understand my desire to please God above all else. However, her gentle eyes had been watching me the past few weeks—watching something eat me up from the inside. Her motive was to restore balance, to stop the hurt; so her advice reflected her desire to help stop the pain. She told me I was being a fanatic. I needed to stop all of the religious stuff, go out with my friends, drink moderately, and have a good time. Funny, but as often as her words had been the balm that had relieved the pains of my youth, that night her voice couldn't overshadow the other little voice that said, "Don't go." I was back to square one.

That night I learned that God has an amazing way of placing other believers in our path when we're at a point of decision. This time it was a lady from my church. Out of the blue, she called to encourage me and to see how I was doing. Great timing! I told her about my struggle concerning going out clubbing that night and about the voice that I had heard telling me not to go. I also told her what my Mom had said. Hoping that she wouldn't think that I was crazy, I asked her, "What should I do?"

To my surprise, she seemed familiar with God's telling people not to do things. She reiterated what God had said. "Don't go." She said that she believed it was indeed God who was speaking to me and that clubs were probably not where He wanted me to be. What a blessing she was to me in that time of testing! With one sentence she confirmed what I had known to be true all along. I thanked her and told her how much I appreciated her advice.

The very next thing I did was to sit down in my apartment and have a conversation with God. I said:

"God, I now believe it **was** You talking to me earlier, so here's what I want You to know. At this point in my life, I have no Christian friends and no social life. I am so grateful to have You in my life, but all my friends are trying to pull me away from You. I don't have any social options, but I am committed to obey You. I commit to never go to another club again."

I heard no audible voice, but I experienced peace in the midst of my loneliness. I believe that peace I experienced was God's way of assuring me that I had passed this test of obedience. In an attempt to display my total commitment to Him, I continued:

"Lord, if I have to stay home every night for the rest of my life, I will. If You don't want me to go to clubs, then I'm done with clubs forever!"

I made that commitment, and to this day, I have never been to another club. I was prepared to live a martyr's social life. I committed myself to follow through on whatever God might want from me.

I stayed home that Saturday night and went to church the next morning. It was strange because I was actually wide awake during the church service. To my surprise, a group of young adults made it a point to talk with me after church. Whether they noticed that I was lonely or just that I was awake that Sunday morning, I don't know. For whatever reason, they approached me and said, "Hey, we've got a Young Adults Fellowship on Sunday nights, and we'd love for you to be a part of it."

Imagine that! The day after I committed to have my social life exterminated if that was what it took to obey the Lord, I get an invitation to the Young Adults Fellowship! That Sunday night my Christian social life began and, almost instantaneously, kicked into high gear.

I don't think that I had a free weekend for the next thirty years or so. God heard my cry for fellowship and rewarded my obedience to His will. I had to say, "No" to my ungodly practice of going to clubs before God filled the void with things that He knew were better for me. No one heard the soft voice that said, "Don't go," except me. I had to make the choice to obey God. No one else could do it for me. Obedience in the little things leads to obedience in the big things. God rewarded my faithfulness with fellowship.

God also rewarded my efforts to evangelize my old friends, the ones I had tried to reach while out clubbing with them. The Lord helped me realize that I couldn't reach my friends effectively when there were six of them and one of me, so He gave me the idea of reaching them one at a time. That is just what I did, and one of my friends—Jerry—came to the Lord a short time later.

I experienced the truth found in Hebrews 11:6:

And without faith, it is impossible to please God, because anyone who comes to Him must believe that He exists and that He rewards those who earnestly seek Him.

I learned early that God is always ready and able to reward our faith when we are willing to obey.

Chapter Two

An Embarrassing Lesson

My first act of service to God was serving as a church usher. Being an usher on Sunday nights might not sound like a glamorous ministry, especially when compared to the bright lights of the disco, but at this church being an usher was a pretty big deal. Ushers wore badges with their names on them. Except for my baseball and football jerseys, I had never had anything else with my name on it. I eagerly accepted my badge and began my new ministry with pride and enthusiasm.

As time progressed, I realized that I enjoyed making people feel welcome in God's house. I loved being the first point of contact for people entering the church. I distributed the bulletins and handouts with a smile on my face. Joy filled my heart as I enthusiastically escorted people to their seats. Serving God as an usher gave me a sense of fulfillment. I wanted to be the best usher that I could be. I found myself arriving at church 30 minutes early and often being the last one to leave. Serving the Lord had an energizing effect on me. God was giving me my first glance at what He had in store for me. All I knew was that being an usher really pumped me up!

One Sunday shortly after beginning my ushering du-
ties, an older lady in church pulled me aside. I had a lot of
respect for this woman so I certainly wanted to hear what
she had to say. Or, so I thought! With as much tact as she
could muster, she informed me that some of her friends
had been talking about the new usher who had been serving so enthusiastically. They all agreed that some of the
clothes I wore were causing these women to stumble. I
had never given any thought to the idea that what I wore
in church would attract attention. I dressed the way I had
always dressed, which may have been the source of the
problem. The idea that I could cause others to stumble by
the way I dressed took me completely by surprise. I wasn't
sure what she was talking about, but when she mentioned
that my pants were too tight, the reality struck me like a
ton of bricks! It freaked me out! I was causing older wom-
en to lust after me! I, a twenty-two year old guy who had
just recently fallen in love with Jesus, was being told by a
woman old enough to be my mom that I was causing the
older women to lust! My first thought was, "Oh, my gosh!
How fast can I burn these pants?"

I learned something very important that day. As a follower of Christ, I need to be careful about the things I do
and how I affect people. I learned that if there is something
in my life that could be a stumbling block or a hindrance
to someone else, I need to be willing to release it.

In I Corinthians 8:13 Paul wrote:

Therefore, if what I eat causes my brother to fall into sin, I will never eat meat again, so that I will not cause him to fall.

Paul addressed a controversy in the church that involved the correctness of Christians eating meat that had previously been sacrificed to pagan idols. He concluded that although the practice was not wrong, if it caused a weaker Christian to stumble, then the practice should be avoided. In my former way of life, I often wanted to draw attention to myself; my new life in Christ called me to draw attention to Christ. I must be willing to give myself away for the sake of others. That day, I made the choice to follow Christ. Needless to say, that was the last of the tight pants!

Chapter Three

Speaking for God

God brought newness into my life by gently cleaning the slate of sin that I harbored in my heart. He was rewriting the story of my life. I believe in these early years of following Christ, God was taking me through the School of Discipleship, carefully teaching me how to let go of my old self and allow His ways to direct my life. The pattern seemed to be: God allowed me to go through an experience. Then He used it to teach me a lesson. Afterwards, He gave me a test to determine if I had learned the lesson. If I had learned the lesson to His satisfaction, we then moved to the next lesson. This pattern continued for many years. (Actually, I am still in the School of Discipleship and will be until the day I meet Jesus. He is still working on me.)

Not long after the "tight pants" incident, God gave me an opportunity—an invitation to speak to the youth and young adults at our church. The Youth Pastor asked me if I would give my testimony to the youth and college students on a Friday night. I remember quickly saying yes. Then I realized that I didn't know what I had agreed to do.

"What is a testimony?" I asked.

Since I hadn't been in church very long, I didn't understand a lot of the Christian lingo. I had no idea what a testimony was, much less how to give one!

The Youth Pastor smiled a bit and explained that a testimony told the story of how you personally came to know Christ. Then I understood and again agreed to do it.

On that Friday night, there were about 50 students gathered in the Chapel Hall to hear my testimony/story. This would be the first time I had ever spoken publicly. I felt nervous but also excited to tell this group what Christ had done in my life. The acoustics in the room were not good. The speaker hung on the back wall, and as I began to speak, I heard my voice coming back at me through the speaker. I froze. I had shared only a few words of my testimony, and for about 30 seconds I stood in absolute silence. Everyone was looking at me. I was not able to say even one word! After my uncomfortably long pause I managed to regain my composure and share my testimony.

Though I was traumatized, the students were encouraged by my story. I was glad God was able to use my story to help these students. Looking back, I understand that God was preparing me for a time in the future when He would use me to speak regularly on His behalf. I'm so glad I didn't give up.

The lesson I learned was that I needed to become accustomed to the sound of my own voice. Also, I learned to trust that God would use everything in my life to prepare me for His plan—even when I'm too scared to speak.

Chapter Four

Prove Your Call

In the early years of my Christian walk, God gave me opportunities to share what He was doing in my life. Perhaps it was because I stuck out like a sore thumb that people began to notice me. I was "unique" in this church, which resulted in people who normally might not have talked to me feeling comfortable striking up a conversation. What made me unique? I was what is known in New York as a "Guido" (a term for a stereotypical Italian). Christ had taken over the inner man, but the outer man was still a "Guido."

Needless to say, there weren't many "Guidos" in the church I attended. My arrival must have amused the church people. However, Christ was present in my life, and even though I continued to look like a "Guido" after becoming a Christian, I was okay with that and with the attention it drew. Although people who didn't know me were taken back by my appearance, I knew I made a positive impact in the church. Many times those who had been Christians a lot longer than I would approach me and say, "Wow! You have this fire inside of you, and it's awesome! What's going on in your life?"

I'd tell them, "It's Jesus."

As a young Christian, I was reading the Bible and

praying a lot. I guess my love for Jesus was showing. People were encouraged by the changes they saw in me. I didn't have the theological words to describe what was occurring, but from what others said, I knew that good things were happening. I felt like a different person inside. I couldn't contain it. I was growing spiritually, and my life began to change in ways I had never expected.

Changes that God continued making in my life led me to believe that He wanted me to leave my landscaping business and go into full-time ministry. I felt tremendous excitement at the thought of being a pastor, and I wanted to share my joy with my Senior Pastor. I set up a lunch meeting to tell him about the new direction I felt God leading me in.

At a Chinese restaurant in Staten Island, I burst out with my news before we could even order our food. I was so excited that I could not wait another minute to tell the Senior Pastor what God was doing in my life. I listed all the things God had done for me and all the things I was doing in response to His call. I shared with him that I felt certain God was calling me in this direction. I wanted his blessing and guidance.

My pastor remained silent. He looked at me seriously.

"How do you plan to pursue this calling?" he asked.

"I intend to sell my portion of the landscaping business and use that money to finance Bible College," I said.

"Are you sure that this is God's plan for your life?"

"Yes!" I told him, a broad smile lighting my face.

His eyes locked on mine as he said, "Okay, Joe, then prove it. Prove your calling!"

I was surprised at his response. I thought I had laid out convincing evidence for my decision. I was stunned. To an Italian Guido raised on the streets of Brooklyn, the words, "Prove it" seemed like a slap in the face. I didn't like it. I fought the urge to retaliate.

I gathered my composure and tried to understand what this man that I highly respected was trying to say to me. Part of me felt this was an inappropriate response for a pastor to give a person being called into ministry. I didn't feel that I had to prove anything to him or to anyone else. God had revealed this to me. Who was he to question what God had called me to do?

My fleshly instincts were tempting me to revert to the old "street Joe." I paused and got myself under control before I asked the Senior Pastor to explain himself.

"Joe, if God has called you to be in full-time ministry, when do you think your ministry assignment begins?"

"When I complete Bible College and get a job as a pastor," I said.

His response challenged me.

"Joe, if God has called you to ministry, it doesn't start tomorrow. It starts today. Graduating from Bible College and getting a position as pastor is merely man acknowledging what God has already done. If God has truly called you to the ministry, prove it. Prove your calling."

I began to see what he meant.

He continued, "Get involved serving and ministering here at the church to the point that all of us can actually see God's calling in your life. Then the church will confirm that call and send you into ministry."

I marveled at the wisdom of his words.

Chapter Five

Things Become New

God was definitely helping me to become more like Christ as He pointed out things in my life that did not bring Him glory. One of those things was the way I related to girls and relationships.

I realized pretty early in my Christian life that I didn't know how to date in a Christ-like way. I knew from my past that the way I had been relating to females did not please God. So, one night I sat down and asked God, "What should I do concerning relationships?"

God answered, "I want you to wait!"

Although that may not have been the answer I was looking for (a simple handbook from Heaven on "How to Date God's Way" would have been preferable), I decided that I was not going to date until I understood how to date in a way that honored God. Do you know how long it was until I felt ready to date? Two years! Looking back, it didn't seem that long. Maybe because God had so many things that He was teaching me, I was too busy to really notice.

Another thing God led me to let go of was cologne. That may not sound like a big deal, and it may not be an issue for you, but God helped me recognize that I used cologne as a way to attract women. I knew God was telling me that I didn't need to wear cologne anymore. So I let it go.

Let me emphasize that the lessons God was teaching me were custom-made for me—not necessarily for everyone. I recognize that He might never say any of these things to you, but I am sure there are things in each of our lives that God might ask us to put aside for our good and for His glory. We must have a willingness to obey God if He asks us to let something go. During this period in my life, there were many small things that had control over me.

I was reminded of the words of Jesus in Luke 16:10:

Whoever can be trusted with very little can also be trusted with much.

Though God wants us to enjoy many of the pleasures of life, He also wants us to be willing to give everything to Him—even seemingly little things. When God asked me to let go of certain little things, by His grace, one by one, I was able to let them go, all to my benefit.

Another seemingly trivial item that God asked me to let go of was my jewelry. There's nothing wrong with jewelry. My wife has some very lovely pieces of jewelry, and God hasn't told her to get rid of hers. (Though I would love for her to sell her jewelry so we can use the money to buy something practical.) But God did tell me to get rid of mine. Actually, God led me to this on a Sunday night in church. I was enjoying the Sunday night service when I sensed God nudging me to put all of my jewelry in an offering envelope and give it away. My jewelry consisted of a gold Italian horn on a gold rope chain and a gold bracelet. That night God showed me that it represented something from my past that He wanted to remove from my life. So I took it all off, stuffed it in an envelope, and put it in the offering plate. I don't know what the church did with it. We weren't affiliated with any local pawn shops that I knew of, but I never saw that jewelry again. To this day, the only jewelry I wear is my wedding ring.

God also dealt with me in the area of music. Disco music really had a grip on me. I listened to my cassettes (yes, I am that old) in the car and the music took me back to the things I was struggling to break free from. I knew I needed to rid myself of disco's influence, but I struggled to let go of the music. One day as I was driving over the Verranzano Bridge on the way home from church, I became frustrated with my inability to let go of my old music, so I threw all of my cassettes out of the car window. It felt great to be free of them. However, that great feeling lasted only a few days.

My radio was preset to all the local disco stations and I began to listen to them. I felt like I was back to square one in not being able to let go of my music. Finally, I removed the radio from my car! No longer did I have the ability to listen to music when I drove. I was so proud of myself.

Driving without music was horrible! It only took a few days for me to realize that one of the reasons we put radios in cars is to silence the constant assortment of squeaks and rattles a car makes when being driven. For six months I listened to the troubling sounds of my squeaky car, but thankfully, I didn't listen to disco music.

When I finally felt that I was cured of my addiction to disco music, I re-installed the radio and began to carefully choose music that lifted my spirit and glorified God. Granted there wasn't a huge Christian rock scene at the time, so I listened to groups like The Imperials, Keith Green, and the two or three other Christian bands that existed back in that day. I was obeying God as He guided and directed me. You see, I was usually alone while I faced the struggle of listening to music that the Lord didn't want me to listen to. No one would have known if I listened to the Bee Gees or Donna Summer as I drove the streets of NYC. But God knew. And I had heard God's voice on this issue. He was speaking His will into my life for my good, and I knew that the only good response was to obey.

Finally, God dealt with me in the area of giving. When I became a Christian, I didn't know anything about how God wanted us to live, so I was also a blank slate when it came to giving and finances. I had been part of the Catholic Church as a child, but I didn't attend very often. When I did go, I rarely listened. I don't ever remember giving financially to the church. The idea of giving was a foreign concept to me. After I became a Christian, the church I was attending encouraged people to honor God with their finances by regularly giving financially to the church. I thought, "Why not?" I decided to give twenty dollars a week.

Now, even though I am sure that God was pleased with this first step of honoring Him with my finances, I am also sure that He knew I could have afforded to give more. I was a partner in the family landscaping business, and we were doing very well financially. But at this time in my life, twenty dollars a week was twenty dollars more than I had ever given. I thought I was doing OK.

Soon after starting my practice of giving, I stumbled across a pamphlet that caught my eye. It was entitled, "Is God's Money in Your Pocket?" I thought the title was pretty catchy so I started reading about something called the "tithe." The tithe was the Old Testament practice of the Israelites giving ten percent of their earnings to the Lord. Our church and this tract were both teaching that a Christian should give ten percent of what he makes to God. After considering this for a while, I decided that if God wanted me to give ten percent, then I'd give Him ten percent. I started giving ten percent of my net salary (after taxes), but shortly after I made an adjustment to give ten percent of my gross salary (before taxes).

In Romans 14:7-8, the Apostle Paul tells us in no uncertain terms that our lives belong to God:

> *For none of us lives to himself alone and none of us dies to himself alone. If we live, we live for the Lord; and if we die, we die for the Lord. So whether we live or die, we belong to the Lord.*

Knowing this has inspired me to please God in all areas of my life. So, whether it involves little things or big things, I take it all seriously because I belong to Him.

The Lord seemed to have an interest in so many areas of my life. As I obeyed Him and allowed Him to shape my life, I was becoming what he wanted me to be. That was resulting in my life getting better and better. Though change can sometimes be challenging, God was helping me to become like His Son, Jesus Christ.

So for me, the early years of my Christian life were, by God's grace, mostly a straight journey. I found the Lord and I pursued His ways. I'm not suggesting that I didn't have a bad day or that I always did the right thing, but I was doing my best to obey what I knew God was asking of me.

You may say, "Well Joe, that's great for you, but my life hasn't been like that." That's okay because this is my story and my journey, not yours. He works out His plans in each of His follower's lives in unique ways. My path seemed to have few bumps in the road at this point in the journey. Maybe yours has already taken a detour or two. Whatever the case, I know God will meet you right where you are and help you to become the person He wants you to be. He has blessings in store for you if you are willing to obey Him. You may not always have chosen what God would have chosen for you, and you might have to live with the consequences of poor choices you have made, but God will meet you right where you are and take you where He wants you to be.

It is my desire that you pursue God in such a way that you are willing to learn the lessons He has for you. Obedience results in a person becoming a committed follower of Christ. Obedience in the little things leads to obedience in the big things, which result in a lifestyle of obedience. For me, the early years of my Christian life were mostly about becoming faithful to God.

Personal Note:

My beliefs in the area of giving have changed a bit over the years. I no longer believe that it is mandated that a believer in Christ give ten percent of their earnings. I think ten percent is a great guide to use in giving, and I personally give ten percent or more to the Lord's work. However, I don't believe that giving ten percent is a New Testament mandate. According to the Apostle Paul, God asks us to give cheerfully, not because we are under compulsion. Since all we have is given to us by God and it all belongs to God, I do believe we should give a suitable portion back to Him. I just don't believe that God wants to force us into giving more than we are willing or able. I think God is more interested in the attitude with which we give than with the amount we give.

Chapter Six

Front Line Ministry

But you will receive power when the Holy Spirit comes on you; and you will be My witnesses in Jerusalem, and in all Judea and Samaria, and to the ends of the earth.

– Acts 1:8

There are places in every city or town that people don't risk visiting after dark. These rough places may require walking out of the way to avoid potential harm. Harlem, the South Side of Chicago, the Watts District of Los Angeles—these are the places a person goes when they are "looking for trouble," as the older generation might say. Staten Island also had places that were to be avoided if a person wanted to be safe.

One of those places was Guyon Avenue.

About half of a mile from the church, the corner of Guyon Avenue was the hangout of a rough group of guys. During the day you wouldn't think twice about the place. There was a pizzeria, a bagel store, an Italian deli—a normal scene on most corners in Staten Island—except for the drugs that were purchased and exchanged there. That was the real business for the guys who hung out on Guyon Avenue.

This particular corner of Guyon Avenue had recently made the local news. One of its "regulars" had gotten in a fight at a bar and was shot in the eye. The trauma had been too much for the young man. After surviving the gunshot wound, he committed suicide by jumping off the Verrazano Bridge. After that, an eleven-year-old girl's body was found dismembered on the railroad tracks across the street from Guyon Avenue. The police eventually arrested one of the Guyon Avenue "regulars" for the crime. It was definitely a tough street corner.

Although that place was bad news, that's not what got me. The part that bothered me was that every Sunday nearly a thousand people drove past this corner on their way to church—our church. Later, that same thousand people would drive past the same corner again on their way back from church. And nobody stopped. Not one person that I knew of ever took the time to tell these guys about their need for Jesus. I was no better than the rest. I, also, had driven past this corner many times without ever giving a thought to the eternal destiny of the guys who hung out there. However, God was doing something in me, and the days of neglect were about to end.

God was moving in another Christian's heart as well. A friend of mine, Walter, came to me with the idea of going out and sharing Christ with the guys on Guyon Avenue. I was excited, and we decided to begin right away.

Now, the sight of Walter and me walking down the street was, quite frankly, a strange one. We would often hear one of the guys from Guyon Avenue call out, "Hey! There goes Howdy Doody and Rocky Balboa!"

Walter was a tall, slender, non-athletic looking guy who I would lovingly describe as a dork. He was a loud, Jesus-loving guy who would walk into a room laughing, willing to share the love of Jesus with anyone who would listen. I was the complete opposite—a short, athletic, Italian-looking tough guy. We made an odd couple. I wondered who in the world would listen to us. Eventually, I realized that our physical appearances really didn't matter. God had put it on both of our hearts to go to Guyon Avenue.

When we started, we had no idea what we were doing. The first night I was so nervous hanging out on the corner that I bought a bagel and some pizza just to have something to hold while we waited for the right moment to talk to the guys. Eventually, we were able to break the ice a little with the guys on the corner and began to talk to them about Jesus. I thought it had gone really well. I felt excited when we left that night. I believed that we had really made an impression. Well, we did. However, it was not the impression we had hoped for.

The guys on Guyon Avenue had a meeting after we left that first night. They didn't buy what we said about coming there to tell them about Jesus. Instead, they believed we were a couple of undercover narcotics officers out to get them and they decided that if we showed up again, they would kill us! We weren't as effective as I had believed.

The whole episode could have gone south in a heart-beat if it had not been for an unlikely ally hiding in their midst. One of the leaders on Guyon Avenue, a guy named Chris, decided to shut down his buddies' plans. With tremendous passion he told the guys, "You'll kill them over my dead body! They have something to tell us that we need to hear! We all need to know about Jesus, and I think we need to listen to them!"

God works in mysterious ways! Without Chris' protection, we would never have been able to share the Gospel with these guys. Actually, we might never have been able to share the Gospel with anyone ever again! I admire Chris' courage in standing up to his friends and demanding that they drop their plans to kill us. Thankfully, they listened. Maybe they weren't a hundred percent convinced that they needed to hear about Jesus, but Chris had convinced them to at least let us continue to visit them.

The next Sunday Walter and I again headed out to Guyon Avenue not knowing about the heated conversation that had taken place the previous week. We just went about the business of introducing them to Jesus. In the end, I guess we won their trust because they really started to listen. The first guy to respond, not surprisingly, was Chris. Next was John, and gradually others among them gave their hearts to Christ.

For the next 18 months, we went to Guyon Avenue almost every Sunday night and shared Christ with them. Word of our outreach spread through the church, and a group of people began praying for us while we ministered. They might not have gone out with us physically, but they faithfully petitioned God to send His angels to go before us. Much of our success was due to their persistence in prayer.

During this time of witnessing for Jesus on Guyon Avenue, I trusted in Jesus' promise (Acts 1:8) that His disciples would receive power from the Holy Spirit to carry out the work of the Kingdom. The disciples were to be witnesses for Christ and to take the Gospel to the entire world. The power to do this would not be their own, but the Holy Spirit would empower and enable them to do His work.

That is precisely what Walter and I experienced—Guyon Avenue was our Jerusalem. Each Sunday night, the Holy Spirit went before us, protecting us and empowering us to be His witnesses.

While God was doing great things in the lives of some of the guys on Guyon Avenue, God was also teaching me some important lessons. God was showing me that He loved all types of people and that He planned to use me to reach all types of people for His glory—including Guidos and Guyon Avenue-types. Unfortunately, there are many people in our communities who struggle to see themselves being part of a church. For the Guidos and the crew from Guyon Avenue, seeing a guy like me involved in the church and on fire for the Lord helped them to consider that Jesus and the church could be for them as well.

I realized that God had gifted me to connect with Guidos, drug addicts, misfits, and thugs—not the types most of us hope to hang out with. However, they are just the type of people who need Christ. I felt honored to be used by God in this way.

In the days and years ahead both Walter and I would have the opportunity to take the Gospel to our "Judea and Samaria," and even the uttermost parts of the earth with the power of the Holy Spirit, thankfully, working within us.

Everyone needs to hear the story of the Gospel. And God continues to send His Holy Spirit to empower and to go before each of us who will surrender to be His witness. We can trust His promises.

Training for a Lifetime

Chapter Seven

Wonderfully Made

Each of us has our own volume of childhood horror stories that have haunted us since elementary or junior high school. Most of us carried a fragile self-image shaped by the perception of how we thought others viewed us. Few of us had peers who looked at us through the lens of grace. Once others began to latch on to the negative labels given out by peers, we easily felt like a hamster on a never-ending wheel. We found ourselves spinning in self-doubt until perhaps one day the real picture of knowing God, and believing God's perspective of who we are, came into focus. It may take a lifetime to get there; some may never arrive at a place of self-acceptance.

I began to reject myself when I was a child. It got much worse when I became a teenager. Teens have a natural talent for telling other teens what is wrong with us. Somehow, we get the idea that we have to be perfect to be accepted. Throughout halls and lunchrooms of schools all over the world, groups of people decide that we are not perfect and that they have the duty to let us—and everyone else—know about it daily. No matter how supportive and loving our home environment is, rejection by peers can scar a child.

There were several things about myself that I didn't like. First of all, I didn't like the fact that I had terrible vision. I had a particularly hard time seeing things at night. I remember walking past my mom on our street one night and not even recognizing her! When I began wearing glasses, I was so happy to be able to clearly see the world around me. However, sight came with some trade-offs, like being made fun of by my peers. I hated having to wear thick, coke-bottle glasses, so I got used to squinting and rarely wore them.

In addition to the not so cool glasses I needed to wear, I didn't like my feet. I remember someone telling me in junior high that I had big, clown-sized duck feet. Ouch! If you were to look in a book describing dork-like qualities, I'm sure big, clown-sized duck feet would be at the top of the list. My feet naturally turned outward—like the feet of a duck. In addition to making it hard for me to snow plow when skiing, it made my legs look weird if I turned my feet parallel. This made me dreadfully self-conscious about my feet. I started comparing my feet with the feet of my classmates. I remember looking around and noticing most of my peers didn't have feet like mine. "Why do I have duck feet? What's wrong with me?" It made me very insecure during my junior high years.

Also, I didn't like the fact that I wore braces on my teeth. In my day we called them railroad tracks. They certainly weren't chick magnets! They were more like chick repellents. But, of all the things that I didn't like about myself, the most difficult to accept was that I was short. Being short bothered me for a long time. It was to become my nemesis. My eyesight was eventually corrected (contact lenses and laser surgery did the trick). The braces came off, and I now have straight teeth. And the duck feet thing ceased being a big deal. I finally realized that I had unwittingly contributed to the myth of having big, clown feet. My father had told me when I was younger that the size of a person's foot would determine how tall they would be. Being self-conscious about my height, I subconsciously bought shoes that were too large for my feet, trying to convince myself that I was wearing the right size shoe, and someday I was going to grow to be 6 foot 4 inches. Once I started buying the right size shoes, my feet stopped looking like clown feet. However the struggle with my height seemed to get worse. There was no cure for being short. It led to developing what's called "Short Man Syndrome." I subconsciously tried to overcome being short by becoming a tough guy. Today, I would be what is called a bully and would probably have been kicked out of school and sentenced to ten years in prison. Being a bully was a function of Short Man Syndrome. I didn't like being short, and I didn't like being looked down on (no pun intended) because of my height. I bullied people as a way of gaining respect from peers and releasing the anger I felt because I was vertically challenged.

As a teen, I assumed that when people looked at me they were thinking, "Look how short this guy is!" Sounds stupid, I know, but this is what I believed. So, I regularly called out anyone who looked my way. In my typical Italian, Brooklyn manner, I'd snap at the person, "What are you looking at? You got a problem? Let's step outside and I'll show you how tough this short guy really is!"

What I was really saying was, "I hate being short, and I wish you weren't noticing that when you look at me."

But, of course, I really didn't understand what was going on inside me. On the occasions when I became aggressive, most people just looked the other way because very few people wanted to fight this tough little Italian. Deep inside, I was desperately trying to convince myself that even though I was short, I was still OK. I thought to myself, "I may be short, but I'll make people respect me."

Though willing to fight for respect from others, I was really fighting an internal battle with myself. Yes, I usually won the fist fights, but I was losing the battle with myself. I couldn't learn to respect or accept myself. I didn't know how. I was the one who had the problem, and no matter who I lashed out at, I was the one in pain. Nothing I did was ever going to change the fact that I thought my height was a cruel mistake.

Then shortly after I became a Christian, something happened inside me that was so radical I never would have thought it possible. My "Short Man Syndrome" miraculously disappeared! My need to be tall was gone. My hatred of being short was gone. My need to confront people because I thought they were mocking me because of my height was gone. I had been set free from this insecurity that had haunted me for so long. The great beast that had kept me captive no longer had any power over me. It was as if God had literally set me free! I looked at myself and, for the first time, saw who I really was. And it was wonderful!

I had always looked at myself and focused on the flaws, but I was led to a passage of scripture that allowed me to see things quite differently. It spoke of the divine purpose of God's design of each of us. This new discovery of truth was filled with healing power. It was from Psalm 139: 13-16:

For You created my inmost being;
You knit me together in my mother's womb.
I praise you because I am fearfully
and wonderfully made;
Your works are wonderful, I know that full well.
My frame was not hidden from You
when I was made in the secret place.

When I was woven together in the depths of the earth,
Your eyes saw my unformed body.
All the days ordained for me were written in Your book
before one of them came to be.

What riches this scripture reveals about you and me. God created each of us uniquely and purposefully. We are not mistakes. The verse that really hit home for me was "My frame was not hidden from You when I was made in the secret place." Now if I choose to believe this scripture, it means that God not only saw the height I would be, but He actually determined the height I would be. God saw my body before it was even formed. My five-foot-five and one-seventh inch frame had not been hidden from Him. My height wasn't a mistake. The Creator of the Universe had made me just as He had seen fit, for His pleasure and His purpose. That meant that I was not only OK, but I was wonderfully made according to a plan from the heart of God. Believing this, I was finally set free!

I learned a life-changing lesson. Not accepting myself—perceived flaws and all—dishonors the God who created me. What an insult to question the Creator of the Universe about how He made me! Think about that. He made every star in the sky, every creature of the earth, and here I was telling Him that He messed up when it came to me. My problem was not with other people and their reactions to me, but it was with how I was viewing myself. You and I will never be free until we recognize that God created us lovingly and intentionally. We are made just as He designed us—fearfully and wonderfully.

Finally, I am free from the agony of comments about my height. Now, when being made fun of because of my height, I will just inform people that I am exactly the height that God intended me to be. I can rest in the arms of my loving Creator knowing He has plans for all five foot five and one-seventh inches of me—just as I am!

Chapter Eight

Grace Given to the Humble

God opposes the proud but gives grace to the humble.
— James 4:6

God hates pride. Many verses in the Bible address the sin of pride. It was the root of the fall of Adam and Eve in the Garden of Eden, and it has also been the root of the fall of many men and women today. I don't think these verses are speaking of being proud of an accomplishment that we've worked hard to achieve, or for a success that we have earned. I believe the kind of pride scriptures warn against is the pride that elevates oneself above others. This kind of pride is dangerous. It negatively affects us and limits our ability to have fellowship with God.

Early in my Christian life, pride found its way into my heart and almost caused me to miss out on some great plans God had for me.

At twenty-six years old, I had sold my share of the landscaping business, packed my bags, and headed off for Bible College. At that point, I was certain that God had called me to full-time ministry. It was a five-hour drive to Word of Life Bible Institute in Schroon Lake, New York, located just south of Montreal, Canada. I should have been prepared for the extreme winter weather conditions. I wasn't! The temperature regularly hit forty degrees below zero. Traveling around campus was a killer! I am thankful my nose and ears made it through the ordeal without falling off from frostbite.

I arrived at Word of Life in January at the beginning of the second of four semesters. I was assigned to Japan Dorm, a half-mile walk from classes. I was given a top bunk in a low-ceilinged room. I had never slept in a bunk before, and I thought it wouldn't be too bad—until I went to bed. There was a fluorescent light six inches directly above my head! I began to think about what I had gotten myself into: I was far from home, out of my comfort zone, walking long distances in arctic temperatures, and now I had to sleep in a top bunk with a glaring light source six inches from my head. I felt misplaced, isolated, emotionally drained, and fearful.

As I lay in that bed the first night, I longed for the life I had left behind. Everything inside me screamed to pack up and run back to my comfortable home. But then, I reminded myself that God had led me to choose this course of action. I decided to make the best of my circumstances. The dorm experience tested my resolve, but there were other challenges to come.

One aspect of campus life I didn't know about was that all students at Word of Life were required to work on campus six hours a week. For me, working was not a problem;

I had worked most of my life. However, getting along with my boss? That was to become a definite issue.

I thought I would be a great work leader because of my landscaping experience, so I signed up for the maintenance crew thinking it best fit my area of "expertise." I figured that once these young men got a whiff of the kind of work I was capable of, they would be thrilled that I had decided to work with them. I knew I had a lot to offer this "rag tag" band of young men. I had no idea how much pride had crept into my heart, but I was about to learn.

On the first day of work, I showed up with my proud attitude. It was below zero that day. I climbed into the back of the pick-up truck used by the maintenance crew with all the other student workers, and off to work we went. The supervisor, an eighteen-year-old, began dropping people off in various spots on campus where they were to work that day. I was dropped in what seemed like the middle of nowhere. He handed me a woefully inadequate tool and told me to start chipping ice. I assumed I would be chipping ice off a walkway, but it seemed that no one ever walked in this area. Trying not to sound too condescending, I asked him why he was having me chip ice in this remote area.

His reply was in the neighborhood of, "I'm the supervisor and you're the worker. That's all you need to know. Now chip ice!"

With that, he drove off leaving me alone with my

thoughts, ice pick in hand.

I began to dislike this supervisor. I thought what I was doing was a waste of my time and expertise. Pride began to creep out of my heart and assert itself.

I thought, "You know, I'm better than this! And I am so much better than that eighteen-year-old supervisor! When I was home, I didn't work for anyone; I owned my own landscaping business. People worked for me! I paid their salaries, and they listened to me. And here I am? Chipping ice for some eighteen-year-old supervisor?"

Needless to say, it was a hard work shift as I wrestled with what I perceived to be an injustice. When the supervisor came back for me, I chose to hold in my growing resentment. I never told him or anyone else how I felt. I tried my best every work shift to be a team player. I did everything I was asked to do without complaint. But that was on the outside. On the inside, an unhealthy pride was growing, and I didn't even know it was there.

Later, my pride was again challenged by my first run-in with racism. Not in the traditional sense with a member of a different race, but concerning my proud Italian ethnicity. Apparently, being Italian was not appreciated by some of the other students. I got the hint when a group of students referred to me as an "Eye-talian"—emphasis on the "I." They used this title as a kind of racial slur letting me know that I didn't fit in. I was surprised. I had grown up in Brooklyn where there seemed to be two kinds of people—those who were Italian, and those who wanted to be Italian. Now, I was being ridiculed because of my ethnicity. This made me very angry. I thought, "I'm better than them! I'll bring every Italian Guido I know up here from Brooklyn and then we'll see who's better than who!"

Pride silently attached another subtle tentacle around my heart. And again, I didn't know it was there.

No one knew that a tangled root of bitterness was growing inside me. I continued to keep my feelings hidden. I never retaliated nor did anything that I thought would be offensive to others. I just smiled and hid the pain. I believed that I was a superior worker and that I had an elite ethnicity. I allowed the pride that was in my heart to fester.

The semester ended badly for me. I ended up in the infirmary along with what seemed like half of the student body with an intestinal illness. The high point of my day in the infirmary was listening to the lectures from the missed classes which the school piped into our ward. The rest of the day was spent sleeping and unsuccessfully trying to hold down food. The isolation, the racial slurs, my anger towards my supervisor, and now this illness—all led me to an angry resolution. I had had enough of Word of Life Bible Institute! I would not return to school after the break.

When I left for break early that spring, I was sure that I would never see that campus again. Luckily for me, I had a wise pastor.

I met with my pastor after I arrived home and told him of my disastrous semester. Although he was sympathetic, he reminded me that the entire church had seen what God was doing in my life. They had recognized God's calling on my life, and he really believed that I was called to ministry. He encouraged me to give Word of Life another try. I knew he was right; I shouldn't give up so quickly. So, even though the intestinal illness continued to affect me, when the semester break ended, I repacked my bags and headed back up to Word of Life.

I picked up three other students from the New York metro area and began my semi-reluctant five hour drive back to school. Within a short time, my three passengers were lulled to sleep by the monotonous highway driving. Without anyone to talk to, I began to think about all the difficulties I had endured at school. Then God entered the conversation. I was getting used to hearing His voice, so it didn't freak me out. God began a dialogue about the pride in my life.

He told me, "Joe, you are proud. You think you're better than everyone else on that campus just because you have a little more life experience than they do. And, you expect that they will bow down to you."

What could I say? God was right. I had no response. Tears began to roll down my face.

God continued, "You think that because you're Italian, because you're from New York City, that you're somehow elite? You're better than the other students?"

God knew my heart. He was right-on with what He said to me. But then came the shocker!

"…and I allowed you to go through all of that mess last semester in order to reveal your issue with pride."

I continued to drive, feeling gently broken, softly crying. God was right. I was wrong. I found the strength to offer a confession to Him. "Lord, I'm sorry. I didn't realize that so much pride was in my heart. Please forgive me. I will humble myself and go back to Word of Life and do whatever it is that You want me to do."

God continued to address something in me. He said, "I want you to go back to the campus and serve the other students. I want you to be their humble servant."

"Yes, Lord," I said.

The second semester at Word of Life was radically different from the first. For one thing, I was finally able to hold down my food. I think my intestinal illness was God's way of getting my attention and showing me that something inside of me was poisonous. God healed me of the intestinal illness and it felt great to eat again.

A few days into the second semester, I was called to the office by the administration. I wondered what they wanted to talk to me about. I was afraid that they had noticed my pride issues from the previous semester and were just getting around to dealing with me. Remembering my conversation with God on the ride back to school, I was ready to submit to whatever they felt I needed to do.

The college administrator said, "Joe, we've noticed that you have great leadership potential. We need a leader like you on this campus."

I was shocked. I thought, "Are you sure you know who you're talking to? I'm Joe, the guy who struggles with pride?"

But the administrator looked me in the eyes and said, "We would like you to become a Residence Assistant."

He went on to explain that in order to assume this position, I would need to move out of Japan Dorm and take the RA position in another dorm. He then informed me that it was a larger dorm with a higher ceiling, much closer to the Dining Hall and classrooms. He said that the school administrators thought I had a lot to offer. He asked if I would be willing to accept the position.

Willing! I was thrilled to serve in this capacity. God amazed me with this opportunity! I thought that He was going to give me a spiritual "Time Out" so I could dwell on what I had done and how I had let down Him and so many others with my pride. But that's not God's nature. He saw my repentant heart and immediately gave me the opportunity to be a servant/leader on campus and have the opportunity to influence other students. Though I knew I didn't deserve this, I was willing to serve in any way I could.

It should not have been a surprise that God honored me when I became humble. In His sovereignty and love, God placed an eighteen-year-old supervisor and a whole group of "Eye-talian-hating" students in my life to address attitudes I needed to change. To be sure that He got my attention, God also allowed an intestinal illness. He allowed all of this because He loves me, and He didn't want pride to have a destructive effect in my life.

I almost missed out on this wonderful learning experience because I was stubborn and considered not going back to school. By attempting to avoid the pain, I almost missed out on the blessing. God revealed my sin, and I confessed my pride. Then He was able to bring change to my life. When we are humble, God honors us and gives us His grace.

Chapter Nine

You Can't Out-Give God

Have you ever tried to out-give God? In my journey as a Christian, I have found it to be impossible to do so. God taught me this wonderful lesson in dramatic fashion soon after I graduated from Word of Life.

The money that I received from the sale of my portion of the landscaping business was used to pay for my school tuition at Word of Life Bible Institute. Once I graduated, I returned home to my church on Staten Island financially depleted but excited about what God had in store for me. To my surprise, my home church graciously hired me as a Youth Intern. I was thrilled at the opportunity and ready to jump into this new ministry. However, the position came with some expectations that I was unprepared to handle. The church required its staff to wear business professional attire in the office.

Their dress code threw me for a loop. First of all, the youth intern in most churches is almost always near the bottom of the pay scale. The pay I received was fair and I had enough to live on, but it didn't leave me much extra cash. I would have to scrimp and save to afford this new "office uniform." I wasn't sure how I would get the cash to buy the required clothes. I had already used most of my emergency reserves, and I was afraid that it would take quite a while to afford the clothes I needed for the new job. I didn't want to spend all of my emergency funds and become financially vulnerable should something unexpected arise.

Secondly, I have always had an aversion to dressing up. I like to dress comfortably and casually. Dressy clothes just aren't something I have ever—or will ever—enjoy wearing. But, it was required. The Staten Island Church wanted their staff to look professional. With that in mind, I wrestled with using my emergency fund to buy the appropriate clothes. I had about one thousand dollars to spend. I planned to buy a couple of suits, a couple of shirts and ties, dress slacks, shoes—everything I would need to comply with the dress requirement for the job. That was my plan. However, God's plans were different.

At church Sunday, the pastor gave an impassioned plea from the pulpit. We were going through a building program, and the pastor felt the church buildings needed to be expanded. It was a big deal for us as a church, and our congregation was being challenged to give sacrificially. I was sitting in church listening. The Lord seemed to say to me, "Joe, I want you to give the thousand dollars you've set aside for clothes to the church's building program."

Now remember, this isn't the first time that the Lord had spoken to me, and most times when He asked me to do something, I responded with a quick and resounding, "Yes." But this time, it was different. I was thinking, "You have got to be kidding me! God, You can't be asking for my thousand dollars! I'm in the ministry now and I need that money because I have to buy clothes!"

I didn't want to be disobedient to God, but I felt I needed a little more confirmation before I made a decision of this magnitude. Essentially, I decided that this time I would ignore God, at least for a little while.

It's funny that when God makes a "suggestion" for your life, He doesn't just let it fall by the wayside. God intends to be heard and acknowledged. God will allow us the right to exercise our free will and not follow His direction, but He wants us to know it's Him that we're refusing.

I postponed the buying of the clothes, just to be safe. A little time passed, and I still couldn't shake the feeling that it had been God who had spoken to me. I must admit that I didn't want to give the thousand dollars for the building program. I had plans for it. I needed it. My ministry depended on it. So I began stalling, hoping God would change His mind or confirm that it was not His voice that I had heard that Sunday morning. I reasoned that I'd move the money from my savings to my checking so that if the voice I had heard was His, at least I'd have the money in a place where I could easily access it. I was making progress, but I was not ready to part with the money just yet. I still had an uneasy sense that God wanted me to give this money to the church. I was not ready to give the money, but I wrote the check to the church for one thousand dollars. I placed the check in my Bible hidden between the pages—trying to lose it without really losing it. How stupid! I was playing games with God hoping I'd win and get to keep the thousand dollars and buy my clothes.

I went through this wrestling match for about four weeks before I finally acknowledged that the voice I had heard was God's. Even though I still didn't want to give the money, it was becoming clear that this feeling was not going away.

God was pretty relentless with me concerning this money, and I could not stop thinking about what I now believed He wanted me to do. It seemed that His voice was growing clearer in asking me to give the thousand dollars to the church. But my heart kept shutting Him out.

Finally, after another wrestling match with God about the money, I knew that I could not refuse Him any longer. Sunday morning, I riffled through my Bible, found the check, and placed it in the offering basket. I had a pretty poor attitude about the whole thing. I wasn't angry, but I gave begrudgingly. I remember praying, "There! Are you happy now? You can have the money!" I had obeyed God, but I was not happy.

That afternoon, my brother Bob was throwing a birthday

party for one of his sons. The whole family was gathering, and it promised to be a fun time. I drove to the party straight from church, still wearing one of the few suits I owned: a gray pinstripe long past its prime. It was a great time with my family, and I promised my parents that I would visit them again the next day at their home in Brooklyn.

The next morning I drove to Brooklyn to spend the day with my parents. When I arrived, I picked up the newspaper, went into the kitchen, and was reading the news. I could hear my dad upstairs getting ready to leave for work. When he came downstairs he walked into the kitchen, looked at me, and said, "Joseph, here's an envelope. I want you to read this, but not until I leave the house." Then he left for work. I opened the envelope and found a letter inside. It read:

Dear Joseph,

Please buy the following: two suits, four pairs of slacks, four shirts, two pairs of shoes, four ties...etc., etc.

Love,

Dad

My mouth was hanging open in shock and surprise. I hadn't shared with anyone about the wrestling match God and I had over the thousand dollars. I had just put the thousand dollars in the offering basket the day before. No one but God knew that I now had a financial need. Now, here in my hand, I had amazing proof that when God asked for my meager savings, He had already provided for all of my needs! He not only met my financial need, but He taught me that I can't out-give Him. I began to weep.

When my dad got home later that day, I thanked him from the bottom of my heart.

"Joseph," he said, "when you showed up at the party yesterday, you looked so horrible in that suit. I decided right then and there that I was going to buy you some new clothes. I intended to buy them in a couple of weeks, but I couldn't sleep last night. About two o'clock this morning, I got out of bed and felt God was asking me to write you that letter. Once I wrote it, I was able to go right to sleep."

Coincidence? No. God waited for the moment when I was willing to let go of what I thought I needed, and then He provided exceedingly and abundantly more than I could have purchased on my own. He used my dad to provide what I was convinced I had to provide for myself. And, by the way, when the shopping spree was all said and done, I had spent well over the one thousand dollars that I gave to the church. Did I out-give God? No! Can you out-give God? I don't believe you can. Does He always respond as He did on this occasion? No, but I've never had a moment when I could not see the correlation between what I gave and what He provided in return.

By the way, you should come to my office sometime. I'd love to show you my dad's letter. To this day I have it filed away. I never want to forget what God did for me when I let go of what I thought I needed. We can't out-give God!

Chapter Ten

Doing Right Regardless of the Cost

Let us not become weary in doing good, for at the proper time, we will reap a harvest if we do not give up.
– Galatians 6:9

Our God is powerful. He created the universe in a day. He parted the Red Sea with His breath, and He raised Jesus Christ from the dead. The Bible is filled with examples of His amazing power at work in the lives of believers like you and me. And God loves to honor those whose hearts are in the right place. For some of God's people that meant times of blessing while for others it meant times of hardship.

For me, standing up for what is right resulted in God busting through my fears and insecurities during my first year as a Youth Pastor. It happened when I took our youth group to summer camp.

Doing what is right often leads to God working through us in powerful ways, sometimes in ways that can take us by surprise. For me, one of the surprises came during my first year as a youth pastor. It happened when I took our Staten Island youth group to summer camp in Upstate New York.

How people can sometimes put on an act in front of

people and then act differently when they are alone has always puzzled me. I want to do what is right because I know God is watching. Pleasing Him is more important to me than impressing others. Though I am not perfect, I truly want to do my best to live a life that honors the Lord.

As a youth pastor, that meant, on occasion, lovingly confronting students when they strayed off the path. But even when confronting with wisdom and gentleness, I learned that the sheep in a shepherd's flock oftentimes push back. This tension set the scene for the next lesson that God had in store for me. Thankfully, I watched God emerge victorious in the lives of the sheep and the shepherd.

After graduation from Word of Life Bible Institute, I joined the staff of my home church in Staten Island as a Youth Intern. I gained experience and confidence in my tenure in that position, and not long after that I became the Youth Pastor.

I had a great first year as I focused on developing relationships with the teens in my youth group. When I considered plans for the summer, I wanted to give the students an experience that would help deepen their relationship with Christ. I decided to take our youth group to Word of Life summer camp, an incredible teen camp on an island on Schroon Lake about a mile from the college campus. I knew that our students would have a great time there. I was excited for them to meet other students; there would be hundreds of teens from other churches across the country. I had already experienced a summer on the Island and believed it to be one of the best summer camps in the area. So, when the time came for camp, we packed forty kids and their luggage into a bus and began what I hoped would be the trip of a lifetime.

We arrived at camp along with approximately five hundred other students and began to explore this amazing Upstate New York summer camp. We swam. We canoed. We fished...it was great! The kids loved it.

Not too long into the week, however, I began to notice some things that bothered me. For some reason, my students were not acting like they normally did. Perhaps being away from home and having a newfound freedom was having a negative effect on them.

The longer I spent time with them, the more I noticed a side of them that I had not seen before. They seemed to be living double lives. Though they claimed to be followers of Christ, their actions and behavior demonstrated something different. I know they were only teenagers, and teenagers do strange things when away from home—especially teenagers from New York City. But what I was seeing was out of the ordinary even for these New York City teens. It seemed as if they were doing just about everything wrong. They were missing curfew. They were missing meetings. They were breaking rules of the camp. The only thing I could think to do was to confront our students and find out what was going on. As I investigated, my concerns were validated. Some of the other kids at the camp had brought in "contraband" materials which my kids were now using. So what was happening was that a bunch of other students at this camp were leading my students astray!

As leader of the youth group, I made it a point to confront my students about what they were doing. Of course, their first response was like, "Oh, come on Joe! We're just trying to have a little fun!" I did not accept their excuse and was determined to confront their wrong behavior. It got to the point where I was spending most of my time trying to convince a group of defiant teens that breaking the camp rules went beyond the bounds of "having fun." Needless to say, the week was becoming a nightmare!

Not long after I started seriously confronting my students, I heard that I was being referred to as the camp "police officer." My arrival at camp activities resulted in whispers of, "Cool it! Here comes the cop!"

No matter where I went, as soon as I got around the students, they seemed to walk away. My youth group students even sat separately from me at the evening camp meetings! I was being avoided like the plague. It seemed like my students and the other students at this camp hated me. The great relationships that I had worked so hard to create seemed to have disintegrated in the few days we had been at camp. What happened?

By the end of the week I was worn out, disappointed, confused, and discouraged. As a first year Youth Pastor, I was desperately trying to help these youth do what was right. I was trying to be responsible, to be a good leader. Yet no one else seemed to value what I was doing. I was labeled the "moral police officer." This was so frustrating. I had gone into youth ministry because I loved kids and I wanted them to know the love of Jesus, not to keep them from having fun. And now, I was being avoided like I had the plague. And what's more, I was sure they hated me!

I couldn't and wouldn't allow them to break the rules. That would not serve God or them in the long run. I couldn't look the other way. I knew I had to continue to challenge them to do what was right. I continued to deal with their behavior head-on. But by the end of the week, I had made up my mind that I was not cut out for youth ministry. I figured I had had one good year as a youth pastor while at the church in Staten Island, but obviously, I wasn't as effective as I thought I had been. It was time to admit my failure and throw in the towel. My vision of being a youth pastor seemed to have died at this summer camp.

As the last night of camp arrived, I was ready to go home and pack it in. However, there was a tradition that the camp had on the last night. Word of Life Camps always ended the week with what was called a "Say So" meeting." All the campers gathered in front of a huge bonfire. If one of the students wanted to share something special that God had done in their lives while at camp, they would stand before the group and share their story as a roaring bonfire created the backdrop. Every camper had an opportunity to "say so" in front of the rest of his or her peers. I at least hoped as students came forward that they would be sensitive enough to keep from going public with their hateful feeling towards me.

On this last night, I wasn't thinking about students as much as I was trying to figure out how I could get back into my landscaping business once I got home and left youth ministry behind. I didn't want to face my pastor, my fellow church members, or my family—but I knew that I owed everybody an explanation about why I was throwing it all away after this miserable week at camp. I was ready to give NASCAR drivers a run for their money on the way home, because I felt like a failure. All I wanted to do was to get home and get away from youth ministry.

Now, by this point in my walk with Christ I was somewhat accustomed to the miraculous, but what God did that night blew me away. Students began to come forward to share what God had done in their lives, and one of the students mentioned my name. Though I was sure it would be in the context of, "This guy ruined my camp experience," it wasn't. The student said I had challenged her at camp, and that God really worked through me to reach her. I'm thinking, "Yeah, right! You hate me!" when the next student came forward and also mentioned my name. Then the next, and the next, and after about ten students mentioned my name, I started paying close attention to what they were saying. Maybe I really had had an impact on these students?

Another ten students got up and said the same type of things over and over, mentioning how God had used me to change their lives. I could not believe this was happening. The students had acted like they hated me during the week at camp. They treated me like I had leprosy. And now I was hearing all of these encouraging testimonies. I began to mildly reconsider my decision to walk away from youth ministry.

Then, literally another twenty or so students went forward and told their fellow campers that this youth pastor named Joe Centineo had made an impact on their lives. Students said that they realized they had been messing up and they were so glad that I had the courage to confront them about their mistakes. While it became a little embarrassing to hear my name mentioned so often during this "Say So" meeting, God knew that this defeated young youth pastor needed some extraordinary encouragement. I remember praying, "Okay, Lord. I get it!"

By the final count, it was somewhere around seventy or eighty kids who came forward that night and over half of them thanked God for using me to confront them about their sin and bring change to their lives. During this meeting, God clearly reconfirmed my calling.

Never before had the Apostle Paul's words in Galatians 6:9 been so clear to me.

Let us not become weary in doing good, for at the proper time we will reap a harvest if we do not give up.

We live in a sinful world filled with bad things. The Lord tells us that we should not grow weary; we should not grow tired of doing good. When we continue pursuing goodness, the harvest time will eventually come. There will come a day, at the proper time, determined by God, when the harvest will be reaped if we do not give up! God was gracious to me during that week at camp, and I didn't have to wait long to see the fruit of my work. For some of us, though, we may have to wait a little longer to see that harvest. Some of us may not see the result of our labor in our lifetime, but we are told to keep at it. What a great reminder to continue to do good.

How gracious is our God? I was ready to quit the ministry. I was ready to throw in the towel and go home. I had given up my dream of being a youth pastor. But God wouldn't let me go! He held on to me when I was ready to quit. I've often asked myself, "Why did He intervene in such an over-the-top, spectacular fashion?" The best I can figure is that I needed epic encouragement to counter what I saw as an epic failure. God wanted to encourage me to continue doing what was right to impact the lives of the students he had called me to serve. Thankfully, He knew that I needed Him to show me that I was indeed effective when I ministered in this way. By relentlessly confronting the students, even though it initially resulted in rejection and anguish, God was able to speak to those students and bring about life change. You see, the battle that week had been His, and so was the victory. All God wanted me to do was stand up for good, no matter the cost.

I still look back at camp that year with a certain twinkle in my eye. God used me for another sixteen years to minister to youth. It involved many a confrontation. I am glad that God taught me the lesson to continue to do good. Many students along the way have benefited from that lesson. I praise God that He didn't give up on me, even when I thought the battle was lost! I learned that doing the good God calls me to, despite the cost, enables Him to work through me to help change people's lives.

Finding a Life Partner

Chapter Eleven

The Leap of Love

Letting go is hard. Do you remember letting go of the side of the pool so that you could jump into your dad's arms as he promised to catch you? You thought once or twice before you let go, didn't you? How about the times when you had to jump off a diving board for the first time, or jumping off a platform onto a trapeze bar as part of a ropes course? Or the time you had to leave the security of a bridge and bungee jump. Letting go was hard, but you did it because you imagined that the reward of the thrill would far outweigh the fear involved in jumping. So it is with love. No matter how much you might want to protect your heart from pain and heartache, there's only one way to experience real love. You have to let go of the fears that keep you grounded and dare to take the leap that love involves. God taught me that lesson as He led me towards the woman I would marry—Toni Capizzi.

During my time spent at Word of Life Bible Institute (WOL), my relationship with God grew exponentially. While I was thankful that God had led me to WOL to grow closer to Him, I have to admit that I was also hoping that while I was there I would meet my future spouse. While nowhere in the course catalogue did they offer a class, "Meet Your Future Spouse," there was a joke on campus that they should have named the school "Word of Life Bridal Institute." It seemed that so many became couples and even got engaged before they graduated. But for me, although there were a lot of eligible young women at the school, I never did find that right person. Quite honestly, I was a little disappointed about that. Here I was, twenty-six years old, about to graduate from WOL Bridal Institute, and I still hadn't found someone to share my life with. While I knew in my head that knowing Christ should be enough for me to be content, I was still a little disappointed that I had yet to find my life partner.

Meanwhile, back home at my church in Staten Island, unbeknownst to me, God was preparing someone for that very role. A young woman started to attend the church while I was away at Bible College. She had heard about me and was impressed. The clincher for her was finding out that I, too, was Italian. Having seen my picture, she declared to a few close friends that, "Joe Centineo is the man I'm going to marry!" Though we had never met, she was sure that I was "the one." Friends at home began actively trying to get us together. John —a good friend and former Guyon Avenue convert—began a letter-writing campaign to me at Word of Life on her behalf. John told me that a new girl at church named Toni was interested in meeting me, and that he thought I should get to know her when I returned.

So there I was, a few weeks after graduation, on a date with Toni Capizzi. I must admit, I had a great time. I loved her pleasant disposition and her godly character, but something wasn't quite clicking for me. Something was preventing me from truly connecting with her. I decided to give Toni a chance, and as time progressed, I began to like her more and more. A couple of months into our dating, though I thought things were going pretty well, I still wasn't quite ready to consider a lifetime commitment with Toni. Honestly, I just didn't think Toni was so special. However, Toni was much more perceptive than I. She made a comment that was to change the direction of our relationship. We were sitting in my car when she turned to me and said, "So Joe, when are you going to let the wall down?" I didn't see that one coming. I was defensive, and didn't have much to say at the time. I really didn't know what she was referring to. I went home that night a little confused and, quite honestly, a little angry. Though I couldn't see what she was referring to, it rattled me nonetheless.

Although I didn't want to admit it, deep down I knew Toni was right. Her question had revealed the reason our relationship was not able to move forward. I was holding back. I thought I was being strong, holding myself at a distance in the relationship until I was sure she was worth the risk. However, Toni's question revealed that even though it had been more than five years since I had found out about my previous girlfriend's unfaithfulness, I was still feeling the effects of that pain. It had been an epic break-up—the worst emotional pain that I had ever experienced. It resulted in my finding Christ as my Savior, but it also resulted in my having a resolve to protect my heart from ever experiencing that kind of pain again. My reason for creating a safe zone was legitimate, but in trying to protect myself from hurt, I had also insulated myself from love. Unconsciously, fear had created an emotional protective wall around my heart—a wall that no one, not even myself—could climb over or break through. I had placed guards on that wall, and they were vigilant in not allowing emotions to cross its borders. I knew that I needed God to help me. I just didn't know how to do it.

That night as I lay in bed trying to figure things out, God brought a verse to me that helped me pinpoint just where the problem was. My focus was all wrong. God didn't want me to climb the wall—He wanted me to remove it!

I remembered I John 4:18 which says:

There is no fear in love, but perfect love drives out fear....

Love demands that we overcome our fears, become vulnerable, and take a risk. God did that when He created man. He desired fellowship with us, so He created us in

His own image. He gave us the choice of knowing and following Him. That risk has brought pain and anguish to God because He has experienced rejection from so many of His created beings. However, that risk has also brought great joy to God in the love and close relationship He has experienced with many who have believed in and followed Him.

Jesus took a risk when He came to earth, became a man, and offered Himself to the world as its King. Jesus was rejected, and hung on a cross feeling forsaken by mankind and even by His Father. But love triumphed. Jesus' willingness to take the risk of loving us has resulted in our redemption.

Was I willing to overcome my fear, become vulnerable, and take the risk to love? The risk of pain was great, I knew, but the risk of not loving was perhaps even greater. It was then that I realized I would never experience the incredible joy of giving myself to someone else in a love relationship unless I was willing to overcome my fear of getting hurt and open up my heart. If I wanted love, I had to be willing to experience the risks associated with love.

God showed me that the reason I didn't think that Toni was so special was that I didn't **want** Toni to be so special. The problem was not with her, but with me. I saw for the first time since the previous relationship ended some five years ago, that I was not allowing myself to give or to feel love. I began to see that as long as I didn't allow myself to go "all in", then even if things in a relationship didn't work out, I could still walk away without feeling much pain. However, this approach would prevent me from ever experiencing the joy of love! That night God showed me that I needed to overcome my fear of getting hurt. I needed to remove the wall and become vulnerable. My inability to connect to Toni was really an unwillingness to connect to Toni.

Once I became aware of this, even though I was still fearful, I told the Lord that I would take the risk of falling in love.

After I made this decision, it didn't take long to fall head over heels in love with Toni Capizzi. Oh, did I ever fall in love with Toni! I took what I call the "Nestea Plunge." It was amazing and wonderful. It was what I had always wanted and had always been searching for. I did not think it was possible to love another person the way that I loved Toni. There were times when I feared that the love I had for Toni was more intense than the love I had for God. I remember praying, "God, please don't be upset with me, but I think I love Toni more than I love you!"

I was sure I heard God chuckling softly as He gently impressed on my heart that it was okay to love Toni with this type of passion. God showed me that my love for Him was different. I learned that different did not mean less; it was just new and different. God was actually happy for me.

It was an amazing time for Toni and me. We both knew we had found the perfect match, and perfect love is without fear. I never would have found Toni if I hadn't had the courage to risk it all.

Chapter Twelve

Until God Alone is Enough

The Rolling Stones became famous for the lyric, "You can't always get what you want." It's true. We can't. We like to think that we can have everything our heart desires, but even if we did, it would not bring satisfaction. At some point, we all come to the realization that satisfaction comes more from a state of mind than from a collection of "stuff." Some people gather lots of "stuff" hoping to fill the empty space in their lives. They believe the myth that more "stuff" equals a better life. The wise recognize that seeking things will never get us what we truly need.

Getting to the place where I depend on God—and God alone—for all that I need has become a goal for me. I have tried to release everything I have, everything I have ever wanted, and everything that I think I will ever need, to Him. At times, God has been gracious and has given me exactly what my heart desired. At other times He has not. Getting to the place where I can be **content** regardless of my situation is where I want to be. God was trying to get me to that place as I sought His plan for Toni and me.

Toni knew long before I did that we would be married. She would often initiate conversations about what our life would be like after we were married. By early November, of 1985 I was certain that she was to be my life partner. I decided to surprise her on Christmas Day with a proposal and a ring. All seemed right with the world that fall, but life took a strange turn for us as Thanksgiving approached.

Neither of us understood what was taking place, but a "stranger" seemed to have entered our relationship. This "stranger" manifested itself in fear. Toni began to fear being married to a pastor. This took me completely by surprise. We had both been on the same path, but now, all of a sudden Toni seemed to be moving backwards just when I was ready to charge ahead. I tried to help Toni verbalize her fears, but she seemed to be at a loss concerning what was happening. We found ourselves searching for answers more than finding them.

Some days she would say, "I'm not sure I love you." That statement stunned me.

"Come on, you were the one who started this whole ball rolling. Don't you remember seeing the picture of me before we even met? Remember hearing my Italian name and knowing I was the one you were going to marry? What do you mean you are "not sure" that you love me?"

Other days she would say, "I'm not sure if I'm attracted to you." Then other times she hurt me by saying, "I don't know if I could marry someone who's shorter than me."

Her fears didn't make sense to me. They were shallow and without substance. These conversations were becoming more and more difficult for me. Her comments were beginning to hurt me deeply.

Though my self-image was being badly bruised, I was still all in with the relationship. Remember, I had let down the walls, exactly as God had led me to, and I was taking a chance, a risk, with love. And now Toni was having all these crazy doubts?

By this time Christmas had long passed, and we were no longer even close to getting engaged. As we talked through the issues, Toni finally told me that her greatest fear was that she wasn't sure she had what it took to be a pastor's wife. Now I'm thinking to myself: Why is all this stuff coming out now? You've been dating me for a year and a half, and it just now occurred to you that marrying me will make you a pastor's wife!

Toni was fully embracing the possible sacrifices that being married to a pastor could require. What might have seemed romantic from afar began to scare her up close. Toni was no longer sure that she wanted that kind of life.

This inner battle began to take its toll on Toni. Her fear was preventing her from sleeping. I soon realized Toni was struggling with depression, though it seemed more complex than that. We didn't really know what was wrong. All I knew was that if this was the woman God wanted me to marry, then I needed to do whatever I could to help her through this difficult time. In my heart, I believed that we could make it through this. I thought that all she needed was a little encouragement. I believed that Toni loved me. She couldn't have manufactured the "look" in her eyes that I saw so often when we were together.

During this challenging season in our relationship, it seemed like each night I had to remind Toni of all we had going for us. I would remind her that she really wanted to marry me, that she was attracted to me, and that I really am not that short. (Well, two out of three isn't bad!) Toni would get to the place where she agreed with me, and it would seem all was back on track. The problem was, the next night, I would have to go through the same thing again. This became a nightly ritual. Again and again, I had to re-convince the woman I loved that she did indeed love me.

There was nothing else I could do. I loved Toni, and I would have done anything for her. I tried to be her knight in shining armor and slay the beast that was taking her captive. Yet, in the middle of the chaos, I began to ask myself some deep questions.

I struggled with what our relationship was becoming. I even considered leaving the ministry so I could marry Toni. So, I had to ask myself, "Am I dependent on my relationship with Toni to make me whole, or do I still believe that God alone is enough?"

I wrestled with that question. Of course, I loved God,

and of course, I loved Toni. I believed that God had brought us together to love each other. But, was I placing Toni and her needs above God's calling on my life? Was I willing to ignore what God wanted for me in order to satisfy my desire to marry her? God had an important lesson to teach me.

As I was reading my Bible, God reminded me of a familiar scripture in the Gospel of Matthew:

> *Seek first the kingdom of God and His righteousness, and all these things will be given to you as well.*
>   – Matthew 6:33

The kingdom of God represents many things in our lives which pertain to our relationship with Him. We are instructed to seek His kingdom and His righteousness first. That is our priority. When we live in this way, the other things in life will naturally come to us. God asks us to have the faith to put Him first in our lives. Only then will we experience satisfaction and contentment. We can count on His promise to give us everything we need. I had to learn that until God alone was truly enough, not only was I not ready to get married, but I wasn't even ready to date! God wants us to have the faith to believe His promises. Then, and only then, can we count on His promises to give us all we need.

Before I could properly share my life with Toni, I had to learn to be fully dependent on God. Because I hadn't learned to completely do this, I was having a difficult time letting go of Toni. I was in danger of making a great mistake, but God was about to step in. For that, I am grateful.

Chapter Thirteen

Letting Go

I've always been good at tests. I was a pretty good student in school, at least when I tried. When I had an upcoming test, I crammed the information into my brain and then took the test. I usually aced it, but then quickly forgot most of what I had studied. However, spiritual tests are a lot different.

We often don't know when spiritual tests are coming, so it's hard to be prepared. When we aren't expecting God to test us, the measure of our faith really becomes evident. Sometimes we pass a spiritual test with shining colors; other times we stumble and fall. Surprise tests and trials from the Lord are never easy. When God tests us, He intends for us to either apply the wisdom He has already taught us, or He plans to teach us new wisdom through the test. Though we may often feel terribly overwhelmed in these situations, God will never give us more than we can handle.

That's where I found myself in this situation with Toni: sitting at the feet of God trying to apply the wisdom I already had while trying to learn the new things He wanted to teach me. One thing was for sure: I was being tested with something I truly loved.

After about five months of Toni's questioning if I was

the right guy for her, it became obvious that she was not getting any better. It was also becoming obvious that I was getting worn out trying to convince Toni daily that I was the one she was to marry. Her doubts about us were now tormenting us both. I was so hungry for good advice that I decided to call my mother. I knew that mom did not want me to be alone in life. She had wanted this relationship with Toni to work out. Mom loved Toni, and I hoped I could count on her to give wise advice.

I asked, "Mom, what should I do? Should I marry Toni?"

Her answer was, "Joseph, Toni is a wonderful girl. But, she's not the girl for you. She cannot be what you need her to be. My advice is that you end the relationship."

Though I was somewhat shocked, I knew that my mother was right. Her advice helped to crystallize the decision before me. I could either be the man God had called me to be, or I could be the man Toni needed me to be. I couldn't do both. I loved Toni, but I knew I had to end our relationship if I was to fulfill the calling God had placed on my life.

A story in Genesis seemed to mirror my situation. It was the story about Abraham—a man who also had a difficult choice to make. God had promised 75 year-old Abraham a son on whom a great nation would be built. Abraham waited a long time for God to fulfill His promise, and finally, after 25 years, Abraham's wife Sarah gave birth to this promised child. They named him Isaac.

When Isaac was 12 years old, God asked Abraham to take his beloved son to Mount Moriah and sacrifice him as a burnt offering. Abraham had to choose between keeping his son or obeying God's command. What would Abraham do? He loved his son with all his heart. Could he ever willingly separate himself from his own flesh and blood? In one of the most amazing demonstrations of faith, Abraham chose to obey God and willingly offered Isaac to God as a sacrifice. However, just as Abraham was about to sacrifice his son, God intervened. God stopped Abraham's hand, yet affirmed him for his willingness to sacrifice what was so precious to him. What a man of faith Abraham was! Read this amazing story recorded in Genesis 22.

I wondered if I was being tested in a similar way. Had God asked me to choose between obedience to His call and the love of my life? The choice seemed much easier when it was someone else doing the sacrificing. I had a decision to make, and I knew what God was calling me to do.

After fifteen months of being in a relationship with Toni, I did what felt like the hardest thing that I had ever done in my life. I ended the relationship. I placed my faith in what I believed to be God's call for my life. Though I knew it was the right decision, I was shattered. I had placed my best friend and my life partner on the altar and ended our relationship. Unfortunately, God didn't step in and stop me like he stopped Abraham. The sense of loss was devastating. Over and over, I asked God "Why? Why did You let me meet her in the first place? Why did You let me love her only to have to let her go? Couldn't I have avoided this pain?" In anguish I cried out to God, "Why? Why did you let me go through this?"

I was in that confused and hopeless place for eleven days. It seemed as though my every activity was interrupted by bouts of weeping and crying out to God, "Why?" My question seemed to be answered with heavenly silence. Though I knew God was with me, my world seemed to have fallen apart.

I spent a lot of time talking with God through my tears. On the eleventh day after our breakup, I continued to ask God "Why?" As I wallowed in my agony, I received a call from a student that I hadn't heard from in quite some time. His name was Dave. I had counseled him while I was working at WOL Summer Camp a few years before. Dave told me that he had just been baptized the day before and he wanted to call to thank me for some of the things I said to him that summer. He spoke to me about a significant conversation that had really made an impact on him. He remembered my talking about my experience in dealing with heartbreak, and he had shared with me his fear of the thought of a breakup with his girlfriend. I told Dave how God had used a broken relationship earlier in my life to bring me into a relationship with Christ. I had told him that I understood the pain of a breakup, but I was sure that if it happened, God would use it for good in his life just as He had used the pain of my breakup for good in my life. I had shared with Dave how the depth of my despair had nearly led me to take my own life, or the life of my unfaithful girlfriend, and how God had stepped in and changed everything. What Dave remembered most about the conversation was how I encouraged him to keep his eyes on Jesus. I assured him that if he did that, he'd get through any struggle that ever came his way. I had felt that Dave had a breakthrough as we spoke that day at camp. It was nice to know that he remembered the conversation.

Apparently, Dave had remembered it all. In spite of my present pain, I was pleased to know that something I said had helped this young man. I was about to say thanks and hang up when Dave dropped a bomb. He confessed that he hadn't called just to inform me that he had been baptized the day before. He had also called to tell me that he was alive today because of what we had talked about. He, too, had been at the point of suicide earlier that year when his relationship with that girl had ended. Dave told me the memory of our conversation had kept him going. He remembered the passion in my voice as I had talked confidently about how God worked His will through my breakup. Dave figured if God could work through my breakup, then He could work through his breakup as well. He said that our conversation had been instrumental in saving his life, and he wanted to say thanks.

Then it hit me! God was using this random phone call from Dave to answer my "Why?" I immediately had an overwhelming sense that God was speaking to me—answering my question and revealing Himself and His plan to me. I quickly, but politely, ended the phone call with Dave. After I hung up the phone, I fell on my face before the Lord. Everything He was doing in my life was now becoming clear. My devastation was because I truly believed God had brought Toni and me together. The breakup seemed to be a divine failure. I believed that Satan was at the root of the problems Toni was having, so the breakup seemed to suggest that Satan had won. When God intervened in my emotional confusion with a phone call, I realized then that God was orchestrating the events of my breakup with Toni. That was all I needed to know. If God was in the situation, then I could rest assured that all would work out for the best.

Prostrate on the floor of my bedroom, I asked God to forgive me for having doubted Him and for foolishly thinking that He had not been working through the breakup between Toni and me. In my confusion, I had honestly reasoned that Satan was the one who had stepped in and destroyed our relationship, but now, I realized that

I was wrong. God used the phone call from Dave to show me that just as He had used past experiences in my life to equip me to minister to others, He was also using the present situation to better prepare me for future ministry.

Going through this intense period of uncertainty and despair gave me a different perspective on how God helps us. Paul's words to the Corinthian church long ago also enlightened and comforted me.

> *Praise be to the God and Father of our Lord Jesus Christ, the Father of compassion and the God of all comfort, who comforts us in all our troubles so that we can comfort those in any trouble with the comfort that we ourselves have received from God.*
> *– II Corinthians 1:3-4*

Paul tells us that when we experience trouble, God is there to comfort us in the midst of those trials. We then have personal knowledge of God's comforting presence to help others wrestling with similar circumstances.

God allowed me to go through the agony with Toni just as He had allowed me to go through my first devastating breakup so that I might be better prepared to meet the needs of people in this broken world. Even though I had felt like the bottom had fallen out of my world, God would use this for His glory to be made manifest in the lives of others. I now had the privilege of taking the comfort that I had received to comfort the hurting world around me. I jumped out of the pit of despair as I realized in an even greater way that God alone was enough for me.

I was back on track, encouraged and excited to be in the hands of a faithful God, even if it meant losing Toni. I could fully embrace what had been given to me from the hand of God, and could also fully embrace what had been taken away. Finally, I was okay, and once again content!

Chapter Fourteen

God's Timing is Perfect

The closing of a door can be a difficult thing. Part of us always wants to believe in the possibility that the door will open again. We hang on to that hope and find ourselves unable to move on. Though we like to think that we are in charge of our own destiny—that the course of our lives is in our own hands—how do we react when we realize that God is sometimes the one who closes doors? We find our faith stretched to its limits. If we could only have God's perspective we would understand His plan in our lives, the beautiful way in which He works things together for good and for His glory.

Unfortunately, we are limited in our earthly perspective and are relegated to seeing life as if it were the underside of a needlework project. We only see the knots and chaotic threads. Life looks messy, and the dead ends seem just that—dead. How will we find the desire to move beyond the broken threads?

That is where God left Toni and me. The door was closed, and I was sure that it was closed forever. Surprisingly, I was okay with God's "No" to our relationship. I had gotten to the place in my faith that I assumed God had another plan—perhaps even a different woman to be my life partner. From my perspective, God's track record in my life was perfect, so I found it easy to trust Him and to let go of the relationship with Toni. I moved on. Toni did not.

When I look back, I like to say that after our break-up Toni came to her senses, but that somehow seems to trivialize the fears she struggled to control. Her fears were real and destructive; our relationship was one of their victims, or so we thought. The truth of the matter is that after five months of doubting and two weeks of our being apart, Toni realized that she had made a great mistake. She desperately wanted to re-open the closed door, but perhaps it was too late. God had touched me and healed me of the pain of the breakup. Now, other doors had begun to open.

I had begun to date a young woman from California who had visited our church while on a mission trip. When Toni got wind of my new relationship she was miserable. Little did we know that God was at work on our behalf. Later, we realized that God had needed to separate Toni and me in order to do some work in her heart that He could not do with me around. He wanted to prepare her for me in a special way. We did not know it then, but my being with Toni put me in the way of what God wanted to do in her life. God had to temporarily move me out of the way. As a result, over the next ten months God was able to teach Toni incredible things that she would never have learned while we were together. God blessed us with a divine "separation" in order to do His work. It would have been much easier if we had known, but like much of life for a Christian, each day must be lived in the moment and by faith. So, Toni and I walked separate paths that seemed to lead us away from each other. In reality, God was moving us back together.

God took Toni through a transformation of her life—her own spiritual journey. She joined a group from our church who were headed to Portugal to minister to Angolan refugees living in Lisbon. Conditions there were deplorable. Toni and the group lived in extreme poverty as they ministered to the refugees. They set up a temporary medical clinic to treat the people there. Exposure to open sewage and a lack of purified water contributed to fungal and bladder infections as well as to lice being rampant among the displaced people. Toni had recently graduated with a Bachelor's Degree in Nursing, and she was able to use her skills to diagnose and help guide her patients back to health. But, since their living conditions didn't improve, the cycle continued to repeat itself. Although the task seemed daunting, with patience Toni was able to partner with the national missionaries to temporarily alleviate the suffering of these people. It was through one of those missionaries that God provided Toni with the vision she would need to become my wife.

Kathy, a dignified and gifted woman, had given up her

life of privilege in the United States to become a servant of God to the people in Portugal. Her contentment with her life in Portugal inspired Toni. While they spent long and exhausting days in the clinic, they also talked, laughed, and shared their personal struggles. Kathy had left behind her desire for designer clothes and nice cars; her focus had become holiness and absolute trust in God. Kathy helped Toni to see that there was a "Heavenly Dream," a goal for all of God's people to pursue. Toni caught that vision. God spoke to Toni through Kathy, helping her realize that there was more to life than attaining the "American Dream." Things Toni had thought were so important no longer seemed to matter. She began to understand that serving God was a privilege, and that trusting in Him should be the pursuit of her life—even if that meant marrying a pastor and living in a meager home wherever God called them to be. It was here, many miles from home, that Toni had her own "Abraham" moment. Toni was able to place on the altar all of the things she had felt she'd lose being married to me. She walked away from Portugal no longer afraid to marry me. Toni came home a new woman: ready for sacrifice; ready to be a pastor's wife. She had become the right person for me to marry.

While all of these amazing things were going on in Toni's heart, my thoughts about being done with Toni hadn't changed. I was still dating the girl from California when

Toni approached me to verbalize her renewed interest in our relationship. I wasn't interested. As far as I was concerned, Toni was no longer the woman for me. However, Toni wouldn't give up on us, and her refusal to give up really started to annoy me. It also frustrated me that all of the wives of the pastors on our church staff seemed to side with Toni. They wanted to see us back together.

My frustration continued to grow during the next several weeks. It reached its crescendo when a phone call from Toni interrupted one of the most important and "sacred" events to take place. The Super Bowl was in progress and the New York Giants were playing! In those days there weren't DVRs to stop the game and to pick it up again later. Her phone call interrupted the most important game of the year! While I was trying to watch the Giants win the Super Bowl, I was being pestered by my former girlfriend about why we weren't dating again. That was not cool! Things with Toni were getting too intense for me. I needed some space—from Toni, from the pastor's wives, and maybe even from New York.

I had been planning to take a trip to California to visit the girl I had met, and the timing for this trip seemed perfect. So, off to California I went. I hadn't been gone very long when Toni and the wives of several of our pastoral staff decided that this nonsense of my dating this girl in California had to end. They all committed to fast and pray while I was in California, asking God to help me see things their way in my relationship with Toni!

For about a week, these women ate little and prayed much in the hope that I'd have a terrible time in California, and that God would make it clear to me that Toni was the right girl for me. They also prayed that the trip to California would prove to be the end of the other relationship. There is nothing like a group of godly women praying that your vacation goes badly! Starving women who pray are motivated and powerful!

The first few days of my trip to California were great. My friend Tim and I stayed in a nearby hotel. We spent our free time with the girls we were pursuing, exploring California and having fun. However, after a couple of days, the novelty of California started to wear off, and I began to notice little things that caused me to take a second look at my West Coast girlfriend. First, she was not Italian. I know it may be hard for non-Italians to realize how important this issue was. There are just certain things that Italians do that others might not understand—things like the food we eat, the way we talk, the way we get together as families in large, loud gatherings. It was becoming clear to me how important those things were and how foreign they were to my California girlfriend. I realized that this could be a major hindrance in the relationship. I also began to notice other things that just weren't working with us. Gradually,

I began to think that this girl was probably not the one for me. I had traveled across the country to get to know this girl better, and now things weren't even going to work out. I was a little disappointed, to say the least.

My mind started to wander as I sat, depressed, in my windowless, economy-sized hotel room. I began to remember how great life was when Toni and I were together. I had really loved Toni. She easily met all of my expectations for a marriage partner. I wondered if there was a possibility that the two of us could get together again. How ironic that I would be wrestling with this idea as the pastor's wives in my church, unbeknownst to me, were praying for this exact thing to take place. All I knew was that I began to miss what I had with Toni. Should I give it another try? Could it work? I honestly didn't know, but I was feeling like I might be willing to give our relationship another chance. When the vacation came to an end, I officially broke off things with the California girl and headed home resolved to seek out Toni.

I arrived home on a Thursday evening, and church services were taking place. I dropped my bags in the room I lived in at the church and walked down the hallway. I saw Anna, one of the pastors' wives who had been secretly fasting and praying for my situation. I noticed that she looked like she had lost a little weight. She was a good friend of Toni's, and by far the most vocal advocate of our relationship.

I knew that she would be excited to hear of my new plans, so I started to tell her that I planned to begin dating Toni once again. However, Anna cut me off before I could say a word. She had a lean, hungry look in her eyes, and this Puerto Rican fireball laid into me.

"Joe Centineo! I am sick and tired of all this garbage! Going off to the West Coast to meet this California girl! You need to get your head on straight! Since you have been gone, the other pastors' wives and I have been fasting and praying with Toni that you would forget about that girl, and that you would come to your senses and realize that Toni is the girl you are supposed to marry!"

As Anna blurted out these words, I was astonished. That they were fasting and praying for this was a complete surprise to me.

"Anna, that's exactly what happened!"

It was like a lightning bolt of confirmation had flashed across my mind. I recognized God's hand at work, and at that point, I had a feeling that Toni and I would soon be married.

On our first date after I returned from California, I noticed that something about Toni was different. With a strong sense of excitement, she shared with me her time in Portugal and the lessons she had learned. Her eyes lit up as she spoke about how she had come to a place where she could trust God in, and through, all things. I couldn't believe my ears! Toni had embraced God in a way that I had always hoped and prayed that she would. I had already come to this place, but Toni had always struggled with trusting God. I realized that God needed to separate us for a time in order for us to both get to the same place. God had created the perfect match. It was just the timing that was off a little. Much like the original Adam must have felt upon seeing Eve, I stood in amazement at God's handiwork in preparing Toni for me.

At the conclusion of our first date, I dropped Toni at her parent's house. I didn't even make it out of the driveway before I knew that Toni and I would be married soon. Honestly, I would have married her that weekend, but our senior pastor recommended that we wait a little longer.

Five months later Toni and I became man and wife.

A season of preparation: that's what I call it. It taught me an important lesson that I have never forgotten. Marriage is not so much about finding the right person as it is about becoming the right person. Becoming the right person means taking the time to mature on your own, seeking what God has in store for you, and pursuing that goal with all your heart. That's what makes you the right person and allows you the freedom to be who God created you to be. Only then, by taking a look around you to see who's moving in the same direction, can you properly discern who your spouse should be. The lesson I learned is that we need to turn away from the world's formulas about relationships and take the time to explore who we are with God and what He wants from us before we choose our life mate. When you are single, becoming the right person is the only thing that you really have control over, because finding the right person without being the right person just won't work. That's where Toni and I found ourselves. We had found the right person, but we just needed a little time to become the right person for each other. I firmly believe that if we had skipped the step of becoming the right person, as we almost did, things might have turned out differently for us. But God knew that. His grace brought us through a difficult time of doubt and uncertainty. And he never gave up on either of us!

Incidentally, I am sure that the ladies of the church happily ate their fill at our wedding reception!

Ministering God's Way

Chapter Fifteen

Good vs. Best

Childhood presented simple choices: would we play baseball, football, or basketball? Our choices were simplified even more according to the season of the year. Of course, there were still arguments among some of us when the seasons overlapped, but for the most part, our choices were easy.

As adults, choices are not always that simple. Perhaps the most difficult choices I've had to make as an adult were not between "good vs. bad," but between "good vs. best." Those are the tough decisions. They require a lot of discernment in order to make a wise choice. When faced with these situations, the wise seek God for wisdom while fools rush in. There have been many times when I have acted like a fool rushing in. Now, I can see that I caused myself to stray from the best things God had in store for me. God taught me a valuable lesson through my foolish willingness to accept responsibilities that did not line up with His call in my life. I had to learn how to best serve Him, and that involved discernment. I had to learn how to say, "No" to opportunities that were good so that I could say "Yes" to opportunities that were best.

After marrying Toni, I gave my full attention to

working with students in Staten Island, NY. Though full of energy and passion to work with students, I readily admit that I didn't have much of a clue as to how to do effective youth ministry. I didn't have a plan, nor did I have any interns to help me out. It was just me and a group of wonderful, committed volunteers trying to reach some of the most difficult to reach students in the country—NYC teenagers. But, I was doing what I was called by God to do, and I was doing it to the best of my ability. God was, no doubt, blessing our youth ministry.

The church where I was serving at the time was full of turmoil. As a result, there was a tremendous turnover rate among the staff. I had my hands full being responsible for the Youth Ministry as well as the College and Career Ministry. When the Children's Pastor suddenly resigned, the Senior Pastor called me into his office and asked if I would be willing to step in and oversee the Children's Ministry, as well. Now, I'm thinking: "Children's Ministry? I don't know anything about Children's Ministry!" I was hesitant because I clearly felt God calling me to minister to youth, not children. However, I wanted to be a team player and there clearly was a need in our church for someone to step into this role. So, I told the Senior Pastor that if he needed me to oversee that ministry, I would be willing to do it. I didn't feel called to do Children's Ministry, but as it turned out, there were some great volunteers already working with the children. Together, we were able to keep the program running smoothly.

I was now responsible for the Youth Ministry, College and Career Ministry, and the Children's Ministry. Soon after that, the Senior Pastor called me into his office and asked me if I would be willing to start an Adult Sunday School Program. It would consist of Sunday morning classes for different stages of married groups. Again, not wanting to seem like I wasn't a team player, I agreed to take on this new responsibility. And again, the people in the church rallied around this new ministry. Somehow I was able to keep all of these ministries going. However, I felt like I was wearing too many ministry hats, and it was affecting my ability to be an effective Youth Pastor.

A pattern was emerging. Not long after that, another pastor suddenly resigned and the Senior Pastor once again called me into his office. If I had been paying attention at this point, I probably would have known to avoid his office. But, I walked in like a lamb being led to the slaughter. True to form, the Senior Pastor told me that the Pastor of Evangelism had just resigned. Again, he asked if I'd be willing to oversee the Evangelism Explosion program. I knew very little about this program and told the pastor as much. He responded by promising to send me to a conference so I could learn about the program and how to run it. Reluctantly, I agreed. The pattern was each time a need arose for leadership in the church, I became the go-to guy, the ultimate utility player. It got so bad that soon after, when there was a need for someone to oversee the Deaf Ministry, I was asked, and agreed, to fulfill that role as well! I had no business stepping in on this one. The volunteer who was leading that ministry was hearing impaired, and I don't know sign language. It had to be amusing to watch this Italian pastor and a hearing impaired ministry leader attempt to communicate. Needless to say, hands were flying everywhere! In a six-month period, I had gone from being a Youth Minister to wearing multiple hats of leadership in a church of over a thousand people. Quite honestly, it was too much for me to handle. In my willingness to be a team player, I ended up fielding much of the team myself. I was completely overloaded and beginning to feel the crunch. That's when God stepped in to set me straight.

As one of the perks of being Youth Pastor of this church, I received an invitation to go to a conference in Colorado hosted by Leadership Network. Leadership Network invited about thirty youth pastors to a retreat once or twice a year. It was comprised of a series of round table discussions. It was believed that if a group of youth leaders of large churches could spend time together sharing vision and strategy, it would result in more effective ministry being accomplished. It was a great concept.

At the conference, I heard about great things many of

these youth pastors were doing in their ministries, and I began to feel overwhelmed, and like I was underachieving. There was one guy in particular, a youth pastor from Detroit named Paul, who made an impression on me. He spoke about an event that he had started called the Pro Challenge. It was catching on across the country. The Pro Challenge involved Christian athletes from local professional teams competing with high school student athletes in a public venue. During the competition, the professional athletes were given the opportunity to share their testimonies with students. It was exciting to hear that many students were coming to know Christ at these events. With the backing of Barry Sanders, a running back for the Detroit Lions, and Frank Tanana, a pitcher for the Detroit Tigers, the program attracted literally thousands of students. This idea resonated with me because New York City is a serious sports town. The students in our church youth group were fanatical NY Giants fans, and if we could get some of the Giants to help us reach students in our city, I knew that God could do amazing things.

I met personally with Paul and told him that I thought what he was doing was amazing. I also told him that I didn't think we could ever pull it off in New York City.

He looked at me and said, "Joe, you're approaching this the wrong way. You are a man of God, and you are a man of faith. Why would you ever say, 'We could never?'

You need to be saying, 'Why not us? Why couldn't we do this in New York City?'"

That sounded good, but after giving some thought to his challenge I answered, "Maybe we could pull this off, but I'm too busy with all of the other ministries in the church that I am presently responsible for to even think about organizing this kind of event."

He continued to challenge me, and I really listened; but I could not see how I could do a Pro Challenge with all I had on my plate.

It was on the plane ride home from that Leadership Conference in Colorado that God got my attention. The plane ran into heavy turbulence. We were bouncing around, being told by the flight attendants to stay in our seats when it seemed as if the bottom had dropped out of the sky. Our plane fell through an air pocket. It scared the passengers half to death. During this ordeal, I seriously thought that I was going to die. Not just the passing fear that comes into your mind when your plane ride gets a little bumpy, but a 'we are not going to make it' kind of feeling deep in the pit of my stomach.

As I prepared to meet God in Heaven, He stepped in to meet with me on the plane. In the midst of the chaos, He whispered, "Joe, if this plane crashes and you die tonight, you would not have fulfilled what I am calling you to do in ministry. I have called you to work with students, but you are so busy being a team player, that you are not fulfilling My calling in your life. Now, go home and do what I called you to do, whatever the cost."

"Yes, Lord," I answered.

The plane ride continued to be rough, but my encounter with God on that bumpy plane ride proved to be life/ministry-changing.

You see, none of the ministry responsibilities I had agreed to oversee were "bad." As a matter of fact, I felt like these extra ministries allowed me to use some of the gifts and talents God had given me and were, in fact, helping our church through a tough time. I was saying yes to good things that were needs in the church, and I was helping further the Kingdom of God in some small way. Yet, even though all of these ministries were "good," they weren't what God had called me to do at this point in my life. I had been so busy doing what the pastor asked me to do that I was neglecting what God had called me to do. God had prepared me and called me to be a youth pastor. Every fiber of my being desired to minister to students. But, instead of focusing my time and talents on my passion and my calling, I had allowed myself to be distracted by these other things. I was unconsciously choosing good things over the best thing. I decided that if I got off that plane alive, things were going to have to change.

Thankfully, we landed safely. That week I went into my

pastor's office to talk to him about my now clarified ministry direction. I let him know frankly that I could not do all that he was asking me to do. We agreed that new staff needed to be hired, but until that happened, I would only oversee the other programs from a distance. However, I made it clear that my focus needed to be in youth ministry because that was what God had called me to do. He agreed. My life and my calling were once again aligned.

God's Word in Ephesians 2:10 encouraged me in my call to Youth Ministry:

> *For we are God's workmanship, created in Christ Jesus to do good works, which God has prepared in advance for us to do.*

It was important that I recognized the hand of God in my life. God has crafted each person with a unique purpose. This verse reveals that the works I do for God were planned in advance. God crafted me individually and gave me what I would need in order to do the work that He has planned. How foolish to allow someone to deter me from the plan that God has for me.

By filling ministry holes that weren't mine to fill, I was deterring myself from the works that God had planned in advance for me to do. I somehow believed that I was the solution to the church's problems. God can take care of

His church better than I ever can. In fact, God already had a plan to take care of the leadership needs in our church, and it didn't involve me. I needed to focus on what God had created me to be and called me to do. I needed to say "No" when opportunities didn't line up with His plans for my life and ministry. I needed to do what was best, not what was good.

Chapter Sixteen

Why Not in Staten Island?

The next year of youth ministry was exciting and extremely fruitful. As new staff members were hired at the church, some of the ministry responsibilities were taken off my plate, and I was able to focus my attention on Student Ministry. With renewed enthusiasm, I jumped in head first. My initial task was to sharpen the existing youth programs.

Weekends in New York City have a potential for getting teens into trouble. Temptation is everywhere. A teen could get into big trouble without even trying. Therefore, instead of offering a Wednesday night youth meeting like most churches, we had our youth program on Friday nights. We thought it was better to have them with us on a Friday than out on the streets. We took a closer look at what we could offer our students as an alternative to the streets and decided that we needed to use the church facilities in a more creative way.

The transformation of our church facility began on Friday afternoons, and by Friday night our church became the best student hang-out in the city. With sports as our theme, we created a whiffle ball stadium in our existing parking lot where lights allowed students to play whiffle ball into the night. We also built an outdoor volleyball court. We turned the Chapel Hall into an indoor hockey rink. We even built a bocce ball court (like outdoor bowling). But perhaps our greatest attraction was an indoor basketball court. In one of the children's classrooms, we covered the bulletin boards with plywood and built seven-foot tall PVC basketball hoops. Any student could dunk on these hoops. That created our ultimate basketball arena! We would send teams of two players each into the room, close the doors, and the first team to get ten points was the winner. There were no rules, and no fouls. It was awesome! Now that I was able to focus my time and attention on the Youth Ministry, things were greatly improving. Our students loved the changes we were making. Many of the church's teens became regulars on Friday nights; our youth ministry began to grow.

Although we were doing a good job of reaching the kids who were already coming to our church, we knew that we also needed to reach out to students in our community who didn't attend church. We thought that organizing the students to pray for their friends would be the best way to help our youth reach out to their non-Christian friends. We came up with the idea of a Prayer Breakfast. We told our students that if they wanted a Prayer Breakfast for their school, they needed to find a home to host the breakfast. We would meet an hour before school started, provide a great breakfast, and then allow the students to spend some time praying for their school and their friends. It was a great success. Before long, we had prayer breakfasts at three of the five Staten Island High Schools. Surprisingly, our church kids began to invite non-Christian students to come to the breakfast. Maybe these visitors didn't understand a lot about prayer, but they got to eat breakfast and see the church in action; and they recognized that their friends cared about them. After each breakfast, I'd load the kids into the church's van and take them to school. I remember one morning as I was dropping the students off for school, a visiting student asked me if we could talk about what it meant to be a Christian. We had an amazing talk that morning, and I had the privilege of leading him to faith in Jesus Christ. It was awesome!

While all of these changes were helping us to have a more effective youth ministry, I also knew that we needed to reach more kids with the Gospel. That's when I decided it was time to attempt our own Pro Challenge on Staten Island. After much prayer, I finally got the guts to make a call to Dave Bratton, the chaplain for the New York Giants. After introducing myself to him, I asked if he had heard of the Pro Challenge. To my surprise, Dave told me that not only had he heard of it, but that he and the Giants had done eight Pro Challenges in neighboring New Jersey during the previous year. I asked about the size of the turn out and was surprised to hear that only about one hundred and twenty students were turning up for each event. I was sure that with a little promoting we could get a larger crowd than that. I asked if he would consider doing a Pro Challenge on Staten Island. Dave was a little hesitant since his target audience was supposed to be the New Jersey area where the Giants played their games. I tried to convince him to come to Staten Island by promising him that we would have a tremendous crowd. I threw out an outrageous number. I promised five hundred students would attend if the Giants would come to Staten Island. He agreed, and I was ecstatic. I believed the Pro Challenge was just what this sports-crazed town needed to get students to hear the gospel message of Jesus Christ.

I got in touch with four local youth pastors in Staten Island, and each was more than willing to participate in this city-wide event. I then went to each of the local public high schools and met with the athletic directors. Some of the schools were particularly adept in certain sports. Tottenville High School was the baseball powerhouse, having had regular success locally, and even having a few players reach the major leagues. Wagner High School had a great football program, having recently won the PSAL Football City Championship. Curtis High School was the best at basketball. I thought I would use the strengths of each school to fuel this event.

I went to see the Tottenville baseball coach and made

a deal. I told him that we were going to be bringing some of the New York Giants to do a rally for the city, and I was looking for coaches. I asked him if he would be willing to coach a baseball team made up of the best baseball players from the five local high schools. They would compete in a whiffle ball home run derby against some of the New York Giants. Not only was he willing to coach, but he asked if Tottenville High School could host the event!

I got the same type of response from each coach I visited. We wound up having a baseball, basketball, track, volleyball, and football team coached by Staten Island's best coaches and fielded by Staten Island's best student athletes. They were to compete against players of one of the greatest sports franchises of the day—the New York Giants! Tottenville High School would host the event in their gymnasium. Everything was coming together. It was amazing to see the students from our church so excited about this event. After much planning and preparation, we were ready.

The big day arrived on April 22nd. I remember sitting in the Tottenville gymnasium with one of my good friends, Bobby, about two hours before the event. I was eating a chicken parmesan hero sandwich and wondering if anybody would show up. At that point, it was in God's hands and we needed to trust that He would bring people to this event.

First to arrive were our volunteer staff and security. Then the police arrived. We took these precautions in case things got out of hand. At 6:30 p.m. the students started to arrive. To our surprise, the students kept coming, and coming, and coming. The excitement came to a crescendo as five of the New York Giants arrived. Howard Cross, Myron Guyton, Ron Washington, and others—all heroes to these kids—were there for the sake of Jesus Christ. What an exciting time it was as Chaplain Dave Bratton, the five New York Giants, our youth group, and I gathered in an adjoining room to pray for the event.

There was excitement in the air as we got underway. Between events, a Giants player would share what Jesus Christ meant to him. After the last event, Howard Cross gave a Gospel presentation, and Dave Bratton gave an invitation for people to trust Christ as their personal Savior. The crowd of 1500, three times our guarantee, hung on every word Howard and Dave shared. About 250 students indicated that they had asked Christ to come into their lives that night! I watched as so many young people gave their lives to Christ, and I thought about what the youth pastor from Detroit had told me. I had to admit that he had been right. I had been looking at the obstacles and not focusing on the power of the One who can overcome any obstacle. When we step out in faith, all things are possible. I floated home that night. It was truly one of the greatest experiences of my life. I knew I was in God's perfect will, and was it ever a rush!

Chapter Seventeen

A Defining Moment

In every Christian's life, there are times that we will face challenges. In these moments, we can either run away from the challenge, or we can face the challenge with courage and resolve to do the right thing, regardless of the cost. I call these "defining moments." They don't come often, but they reveal who we are and they shape who we will become. I found myself facing such a moment just after the Pro Challenge.

The night of the Pro Challenge was an amazing night for me—one of the greatest ministry experiences of my life. I was so excited at what God had done, and the thought that He used me as a catalyst for this event was both encouraging and humbling. I was on a spiritual high, to say the least. As I settled down in bed that night, I thanked God for what He had done in our city and for allowing me to be a part of it. I couldn't wait to begin the process of following up on the students who had received Christ and to keep moving forward as we tried to reach our city with the Gospel.

The next day I was still flying high when the Senior Pastor of my church called me into his office. I should have known better than to answer that call. I walked into his office, totally unprepared for what was about to take place. He had attended the Pro Challenge, but due to the busyness of the evening, we didn't get a chance to talk. I entered his office imagining him being proud of me and being excited about the awesome work of God that had been accomplished. I thought he and I would do a little celebrating, a little debriefing, and then we would talk about how to use the momentum of the Pro Challenge to start planning our next city-wide outreach event. Maybe our event inspired him and he had an idea for an outreach event that would focus on children or even adults. However, the meeting went in a different direction than I imagined. He started the conversation by telling me he thought that the Pro Challenge went "reasonably" well. That seemed like a bit of an understatement to me, but no big deal. However, what happened next really threw me for a loop. My Pastor told me that while the Pro Challenge was a good thing for the kingdom, it wasn't of much benefit to our church. I was thrown for an even bigger loop when he told me he didn't want me spending my time doing city-wide events anymore.

It took a few seconds for his words to sink in and for me to process what I had heard. As I reflected on his words, I began to feel very angry. What I thought I was hearing him say was that though the Pro Challenge had been a great success for God and for the kingdom of God, it didn't accomplish enough for our church. I also thought I was hearing him say that I needed to spend my time and energy building our local church and needed to stop spending my time on things that build the kingdom. I could not believe what I was hearing. How could a man of God come to such a conclusion? I knew that this was a defining moment for me. I could submit to what he was saying, follow his leadership, and accept the limitations he was imposing on me. But, that would result in my neglecting God's call in my life. By accepting these terms, I would be turning from what God had called and equipped me to do. This was truly a defining moment in my life and ministry. Knowing that what I was about to say could be costly, I looked my pastor square in the eye and said, "I quit!" And with a little added Italian gusto, I reminded him that I worked for the King and not for him or our church.

In this defining moment, I had done the right thing! Though I had proven over the years that I was more than willing to serve the church, if serving the church stood in the way of serving my King and His kingdom, I could not continue in that role. Put in the position where I had to choose, I would choose serving God and His kingdom. By God's grace, in this defining moment, I faced the challenge with courage and resolve. I did what I believed was the right thing, regardless of the cost. I walked out of his office and headed home.

Now, what I haven't told you is that by this time our family had expanded. Toni and I had two young children. Christopher was two, eating us out of house and home, and Brianna had just been born. Considering the fact that I had never applied for a ministry position before and didn't have a resumé or a plan, Toni was not as enthusiastic about my sudden decision to quit. Quite honestly, I didn't know what we were going to do financially, but I did know that I couldn't compromise and work at that church any longer. I had to obey God's call in my life, regardless of the cost, and I could not serve a church that placed its own mission above the mission of building God's kingdom. Though I was very aware of my responsibility to provide for my family, I knew that quitting had been the right thing to do.

The book of Acts records the early days of the church. After Jesus ascended into heaven, the Holy Spirit was poured out upon believers in Jerusalem, and the church was born. Not surprisingly, the gospel began to spread rapidly across the world. The Jewish religious leaders didn't like the fact that the Gospel was being embraced by so many people, so they arrested Peter and John, threatening to keep them imprisoned if they did not stop talking about Jesus.

In Acts 4:18-20, it says:

Then they called them in again and commanded them

not to speak or teach at all in the name of Jesus. But Peter and John replied, "Judge for yourselves whether it is right in God's sight to obey you rather than God, for we cannot help speaking about what we have seen and heard.

Although the Pharisees insisted that Peter and John stop teaching about Jesus, they were going to obey God no matter the cost. That is exactly what these two disciples and countless others have been doing ever since—following God's directive and His leading to preach the Gospel to the entire world. Some have paid a great price, experiencing persecution, beatings, and even death. True followers of Jesus will continue to preach the Gospel—regardless of the cost.

Though I didn't feel like my life was being threatened, I felt like I was in a similar situation. I was unwilling to let anyone or anything stop me from doing what I believed God was calling me to do, even if it was coming from a church leader that I loved and respected. I had already settled that issue on a bumpy plane ride. I chose to obey God and to do what He had called me to do, no matter the cost. I didn't know what was ahead, but I knew that I could not waiver on this.

Perhaps this type of situation was what caused Toni to fear being married to a pastor. But, she learned her lessons

well. Toni had no fear through this ordeal. She supported me through this situation fully and completely, and for
that I commend and thank her.

Chapter Eighteen

A Mystery

Many people like mysteries. CSI and Law & Order have large viewing audiences as a testimony to this. Watching a mystery from the comfort of our homes can be great entertainment, but when we find ourselves in the mystery, it no longer feels enjoyable. In fact, it can be downright scary.

That's where I found myself after suddenly quitting my job as youth pastor. My life felt a bit like a mystery, and I became a little scared. God was taking me on this journey, but He wasn't showing me how things would turn out. I knew from my history with God that He could be trusted to guide me in these types of situations; nevertheless, I still felt anxious and somewhat afraid. God used this experience to teach me a great lesson: even in times when we may not hear the voice of God, He has the ability to guide us in other ways. When our desires line up with His desires, we need only to follow our hearts, knowing that the desires of our heart will lead us to His will for our lives. I found this to be true after leaving the church in Staten Island and by following an open door that led to a great church in San Diego, California.

When most of us think of San Diego, we think of 75

degrees, beaches, mountains, year-round sports, and—of course—Sea World. However…that's not the part of San Diego where God called me to minister. The church where God sent me was in a suburb called Lemon Grove, and Lemon Grove was on gang turf. I was hired by Skyline, a church of about 3,500 people, to work exclusively with the Youth Ministry. John Maxwell was the pastor of this church, and it was a great opportunity for me to work with one of the world's great teachers of leadership. Also, I had the privilege of stepping into a youth ministry in transition and had the opportunity to build something significant for God.

Though God had led me to one of the most beautiful places in the world, he also allowed me to work in one of the tougher areas of the city—a good place for a youth pastor raised on the streets of Brooklyn. In the course of ministering to the students in Skyline Church, God put me in a position to reach out to gang members within the community. Though I wasn't expecting this, perhaps I should have, given the time I spent on Guyon Avenue. Of course, gang kids weren't the only focus of our ministry in San Diego, but a good amount of time and energy went towards ministering to these troubled youth. Needless to say, these students energized me.

We accidentally stumbled into gang ministry soon after painting our youth building. It was not on the church property, but was a stand-alone building just across the street from the church. We had named our youth ministry "Living Proof" and had painted our name and logo on the building. Shortly thereafter, our building got "tagged." Getting "tagged" is when a gang paints their symbols on a building claiming it as a part of their territory. I didn't think getting tagged was an aggressive move against our youth ministry. I'm not even sure at this point if the gangs knew we were associated with a church. It was more of a warning to rival gangs not to come on this turf.

We painted over the tag, but shortly after, we were tagged again. By this time, I was pretty sure that they didn't know Living Proof was a church youth group, and I believed that if they realized we were a church, they would probably stop tagging our building. I decided to paint a cross on top of the building. To my delight, our building was never tagged again. Not only did they not tag us, but shortly after painting the cross, an assortment of gang kids started coming to our youth service on Sunday mornings.

As we developed relationships with these youth, it became obvious that they were searching for love and acceptance, and possibly, a way out of the tough world where they had become entangled. Before long, we began to have youth from other gangs attend as well. We now had the unique situation of rival gang members attending the same youth service. Thankfully, they usually sat on opposite sides of the room, as far away from each other as they could get. That was probably a really good thing, because these gangs were violent. In our youth worker meetings, we often talked about preparing for the worst—like a fight or a shooting during the youth service. The possibility of this type of violence weeded out some of the less committed youth workers. Thankfully, we never had an altercation. At times, the gang kids seemed to be more interested in the sermon than some of our regular church kids.

To our delight, some of these gang kids began to give their lives to Christ. One of the first gang members to accept Christ was a young man from a gang in a town called Santee. After deciding to trust Christ as his Savior, he asked for a personal meeting with me. His question was, "What do I do now that I have become a Christian?"

I gave him the standard answer: read the Bible, pray, come to church, and look for opportunities to share your faith with your friends; the typical things we tell new believers to do.

The young man looked at me and said, "Joe, you don't understand. I'm not asking about what I should do to become a better Christian, I'm asking, "How do I survive becoming a Christian?"

He went on to explain that as a gang member, he was "beaten in" to join the gang. He would have to be beaten again if he wanted to get out. He told me that sometimes you don't survive the beating. That's what he meant when he asked, "Now, what do I do?"

I was a little taken back. I had no idea what it would cost this young man to leave his gang to become a follower of Christ. I realized that there was no easy answer for him. I thought I should probably emphasize the part about praying. We prayed together there and I asked God to protect him as he took his next steps forward.

I have to say that God was really gracious to the gang kids that came to our church. By His grace, those that wanted to leave their gang affiliations were allowed to do so without experiencing physical harm. They were tough, courageous kids, and I loved working with them.

While I loved the challenges of ministry in San Diego, it was also a lot of work, and the time involvement began to take a toll on my family life. An eighty-hour work week was great for the students that I ministered to, but not so great for my own wife and children. The job was beginning to interfere with fulfilling my priorities of being a good husband to my wife and a good father to my children. I began to realize that something had to give.

I also recognized that California and I didn't fit that well together. California is a great place. Who could complain about the ascetic beauty, the wonderful weather, and the free-spirited, laid-back people? But, I am neither laid-back, gnarly, rad, nor a surfer. I'm a New Yorker, and New

Yorkers are tough, intense, and passionate. I had to work hard to connect with these culturally different students. For example, when I preach I normally get very excited. The veins in my neck have been known to stick out, my voice has been known to rise, and I have been known to get pretty excited. That is my way of getting my passion across to the audience; but, most of the California youth didn't respond well to my style. They liked people who were "gnarly" and "way cool" and "laid back". I had to learn to limit the expression of my passion in order to connect with these students. I didn't feel that I could let loose and be myself and still be effective, because who I am didn't naturally connect with who they were. This made things challenging for me.

Here I was, working in a great church with a great pastor, leading a great ministry, yet feeling that I really didn't fit in. Additionally, I was sacrificing my family for this ministry. I began to think that maybe my tenure in San Diego was coming to an end. I talked it over with Toni. We decided to tell God our feelings about wanting to leave San Diego, primarily because of our unwillingness to sacrifice our family for the ministry. Together, we asked God to lead us and to direct our lives according to His will. We told no one what we were praying about because we didn't know if it was what God wanted for us. Part of me really didn't want to let go of the ministry at Skyline; another part of me felt it was time to move on. Stay in San Diego or move on? A mystery. We looked to God to solve this mystery for us.

I wrestled with this for a while. I wasn't at a place where I had peace about the decision either way. I certainly didn't want to get ahead of what God had planned for me, but it seemed like God was closing the door in San Diego. As tension mounted, I continued to patiently pray and ask the Lord to show me what He wanted me to do. About two months later, I was surprised during my prayer time one morning when at last, a profound sense of peace came over me. I finally sensed that the Lord was releasing me from the ministry at this San Diego church. I wanted to make sure that I was getting this right, so in that same prayer time, I asked the Lord to confirm what I was feeling.

At that moment, the phone rang. A friend that I hadn't heard from in about five years was calling. Brad said he had been trying to track me down for the past few weeks because he was on the search committee for a church in Texas. He wanted to know if I would consider applying to be their new Youth Pastor. I remember thinking: "Wow! That was a quick confirmation." Then, I also thought, "No way is this Yankee moving to Texas!"

Brad asked if I had a resumé. I didn't have one prepared at this time since I hadn't felt the go-ahead from the Lord to leave San Diego. Brad asked if the Senior Pastor at the church in Texas could give me a call. I said "yes" with my lips, but I was sure that Texas was no place for this New Yorker.

When I hung up, I believed God had emphatically confirmed that He was giving me permission to leave San Diego. I was also emphatically sure that Texas would never be the place for me.

But the mystery was not over just yet! I knew that God had released me from the church in San Diego, but I didn't know where He was calling me to serve. Later that week Randy, the Senior Pastor from the church in Texas, called. He was impressed with the fact that I worked with John Maxwell at this well-known and great church. He all but offered me a job during our first phone call. I mildly began to consider Texas. After a few more phone calls, I went to Texas for a visit. To my surprise, I loved the town of Arlington! I also loved Pantego Bible Church. They informed me that they were prepared to offer me the job.

Soon after the offer in Texas, I received another offer from my former church on Staten Island. The Senior Pastor of the church called and humbly apologized for the way he had handled things with me concerning the Pro Challenge and my desire to reach the city. He realized that he had made a mistake in trying to hinder me from serving the kingdom, and he asked me to come back to be their Youth Pastor once again.

The plot had thickened. Two job offers in two very different parts of the country—and no one except God and Toni knew that I was even looking for another position. Though I had clear confirmation that God had released me from the church in San Diego, I didn't know which of these positions He wanted me to take. I asked Toni where she wanted to go. A part of her wanted to go back to New York, mostly because our family was there, but she, too, loved Arlington and Pantego Bible Church. She was willing to go wherever the Lord was leading.

I called the Senior Pastor in New York and told him that I was considering another position in Texas. If he was serious about my coming back, he'd have to fly us out quickly for an interview. Toni and I had told the Lord if he showed us the church He wanted us to serve in; we would follow His lead.

We flew to New York, and the Senior Pastor officially offered me the job of Youth Pastor promising to let me run a kingdom-focused youth program. Now what?

On the way back to California, we arranged a layover at DFW airport, and spent the afternoon in Arlington, Texas. The church in Texas hosted us and we spent some time touring their lovely town. We also took time to review the events of the previous weeks and marveled that on the heels of our having felt peace about leaving San Diego— without ever letting anyone know we were considering leaving—I had received two job offers as confirmation that God was moving us. However, neither Toni nor I had any idea which church God wanted me to choose. As we sat in a Mexican restaurant contemplating our decision, we realized that in our hearts we both wanted to go to Texas. But, we didn't know what God wanted us to do. It was a mystery I could not seem to sort out.

Neither Toni nor I ever sensed a direct call either to New York or to Texas. So how did we decide?

While spending time with the Lord and asking Him to show me where we should go, He reminded me of this scripture:

Delight yourself in the Lord and He will give you the desires of your heart.
– Psalm 37:4

I was sure that God was speaking to me when He reminded me of this verse. I believe that this verse gave us the key to solve the mystery. When we delight ourselves in Him, when we desire to fulfill His will and plan for our lives, then He will cause us to want what He wants us to have. He will give us the desires of our hearts. The things our hearts desire will be the things He wants us to have. With this new understanding, and facing two choices, we followed our hearts—right to Arlington, Texas.

My years in youth ministry at Pantego Bible Church in Arlington, Texas, were by far the greatest youth ministry years of my life. I was blown away by what God did with that youth ministry. You will read more about this in Chapter Twenty-one. The mystery was solved. God had already written our next step in my heart. I just needed to learn how to recognize it.

God hadn't finished with me yet. Although I had earned my degree from God's School of Discipleship, had received Training for a Lifetime, had found My Life Partner, and had learned to Minister God's way, God had more advanced material to teach me for a degree from His School of Brokenness. It would be a humbling education.

The School of Brokenness
Part I

Chapter Nineteen

Prayer Walking

The School of Brokenness is vital to a leader's continued preparation for ministry. Completion of the course work qualifies him or her to be effectively used by God. There is no tuition for enrollment. The student is almost always unaware of the course work that will be covered. Each experience is custom-made for each individual student. If participants could know their specific course work in advance, they would probably choose not to enroll. Most prior lessons learned in the School of Discipleship must be applied in this course. In fact, those lessons will be one's means of survival. Suffering is like the final test at the end of a semester.

As you know, I attended Word of Life Bible Institute for one year and then graduated from Northeastern Bible College with a degree in Pastoral Studies. At Word of Life, they were serious and rigorous in their approach to the students' spiritual life. Students were not allowed to watch TV or listen to non-Christian music on campus. In addition, there was a "No Physical Contact" rule in effect which prohibited guys and girls having any physical contact. If a guy so much as tapped a girl on the shoulder, he would be "written up." I thought the rule was a little over the top, but I felt that I could handle it for one year. They were heavy on the rules because they wanted their students to be a cut above. Despite the strict atmosphere, I really loved my year there.

They wanted us to develop the habit of spending time with God, so they required that each student have a daily quiet time. It was not a suggestion; it was a mandate. A thirty-minute period was set aside early in the mornings when the entire student body had to be at their desks using the "Word of Life Quiet Time Diary." It included a short scripture to read, questions to answer, and a time of prayer. If you weren't at your desk at the appointed time, you were "written up." Needless to say, I got in the habit of having a Quiet Time each day.

Apparently, this was a great way to establish a habit. Years later, I was still having a thirty-minute quiet time with God every morning. I always woke up 30 minutes early to have my quiet time. The only problem was that sometimes my quiet time was a little too quiet. I often fell in and out of sleep during this ritually appointed prayer time. Sometimes, I would wind up praying for two minutes and sleeping for 28 minutes. This was the nature of my prayer life for 7 years while in New York as a youth pastor, and for 3 years while in San Diego as a youth pastor. It even continued into my time as a youth pastor in Texas. I am ashamed to say that I was a veteran youth pastor with the worst devotional life imaginable. It wasn't that I didn't set aside the time, or that I didn't want to pray, but I just couldn't stay awake! When I closed my eyes, my body wanted to sleep, and that's exactly what was happening every morning. I felt terribly guilty about this and carried lots of private shame about my inability to stay awake when I prayed. Although I scheduled my quiet time every day, my prayer life was pathetic.

While pastoring in Texas, I was meeting with a young man from our church, and we were going through a workbook called Experiencing God by Henry Blackaby. In one of the lessons, he suggested taking a 30-minute Prayer Walk during which the participant would walk and pray. I wasn't very excited about this, but I decided to give it a try. My first prayer walk was amazing! I didn't fall asleep even once. I found myself emotionally moved as I walked and admired God's creation. Looking at trees, grass, homes, and animal life made me think about the greatness of God.

That first Prayer Walk was such a great experience that I continued to do Prayer Walks. It got to the point that Prayer Walking became a way for me to wonderfully and effectively connect with God. I gave up the early morning, laying-in-the-bed-Quiet Time and adopted Prayer Walking as my new and improved way to connect with God. Instead of going into my office each morning when I arrived at church, I would go on a prayer walk for about an hour. On days that I didn't work, I went out late at night, sometimes at one or two o'clock in the morning, walking and praying. This was the new way that I had my quiet time, and not surprisingly, I never fell asleep while walking. I found that God often spoke to me in general ways, but occasionally, I would actually hear from God. He'd whisper something into my ear, usually related to the youth ministry I was leading. It was awesome!

During this special time in my spiritual life, Jeremiah 29:13 became very important to me. It says:

"You will seek me and find me when you seek me with all your heart."

Although in this scripture from the book of Jeremiah God was speaking to the nation of Israel who had been exiled to Babylon because of their constant rebellion and disobedience, I know that this verse was also speaking to me. God is found by those who put forth the effort to find Him. Though I meant well, my morning quiet times were stale, dry, and useless. Now, Prayer Walking helped me seek God with all of my heart as I had always desired. I was able to talk to God and to sense His presence. This would become a useful tool while I was enrolled in the School of Brokenness.

Chapter Twenty

Meeting God on Mount Helix

Some things are true, but we find them hard to admit. For instance, during the 70's I had a difficult time admitting that the Yankees were a really bad team. True, but hard to admit. Or, the fact that I would never reach my goal of being a professional athlete. True, but hard to admit. Or, the reality that bad things often happen to good people. True, but hard to admit. Or, the fact that God uses pain, suffering, and brokenness to help us grow and to take us deeper in our walk with Him. True, but hard to admit. I don't like the fact that suffering and brokenness are often the greatest tools that God uses to make us into the men and women He wants us to be. But, I believe it is true.

Trials come in many sizes and shapes: broken relationships, homes flooded, jobs lost, financial crisis, health problems. There are so many things that take place in life that can be considered "trials." But, God tells us in James 1:2 to "consider it pure joy" when we face trials, because God often allows trials to help us get closer to Him.

God had closed the door to ministry in San Diego and had opened up a door of ministry in Texas at Pantego Bible Church. I was with my family in beautiful Arlington, Texas, doing youth ministry and loving it. My family loved

Texas as well. We had recently had our third child, JoJo, and had bought a home. Things were going great. I was loving life, loving the people I worked with, loving the hot Texas weather. I loved everything about Texas and was living out my ministry dream. The youth ministry was really flourishing—life was good. But then God allowed a trial to affect my life and touch my family, which was not very much fun. This is not easy to talk about. Let me explain.

It was January of 1995, just after my family returned home from a Young Life ski trip to Colorado when my wife began to become ill. This was not a physical illness, but rather an emotional/mental illness. This illness would wind up afflicting her over a nine-month period.

Toni had talked to me about feeling a little down and low while we were in Colorado. Shortly after we returned from the ski trip, she started to get seriously depressed. Toni quickly got to the place that she wasn't able to function as a wife or a mom. She wound up staying in bed the majority of the day for about nine months. In the beginning, I talked to Toni and tried to help her get through her sadness. I assured her that this would pass, and everything would be OK. As a man, I was sure that I could "fix" Toni and help her through this emotional bump in the road. These encouragement sessions became daily counseling sessions, and they began to bring back memories.

It seemed that each day I would counsel Toni through

her sadness only to have to do it again the next day, and the next day, and the next day. This became really tough since I was busy working at the church and we had 3 young children to care for. JoJo was about a year old, Brianna was 4, and Chris was 6. And Toni couldn't get out of bed. Thankfully, our church stood by us and helped. They were wonderful. The people in our church provided meals, cleaned our house, and even did our laundry. But even with their help, the juggling act of taking care of Toni, taking care of my children, and leading the youth ministry became more than I could handle. The church even hired a nanny to take care of the kids so that I could continue doing ministry. Despite all the help, I felt overwhelmed. The emotional toll weighed me down.

Toni's mom was also a big help to us. She would spend a week in Texas helping around the house and caring for Toni, and then go back to New York for a week. Toni's mom was such an encouragement and a help to me that when she would leave, I wanted to cry because I needed her help so desperately. It was an overwhelming time. All of us were worn out.

Though I am writing about my brokenness and my suffering, Toni was the one who was really suffering. We were trying everything to help Toni get better. She was seeing a Christian psychiatrist and was on multiple medications. We even suspected that this could be a demonic attack on

Toni and my family, so there were people in the church who engaged in Spiritual Warfare prayer with us and on our behalf. Many people in the church were praying for Toni. The church elders came to our home and anointed Toni with oil and prayed for her. On two different occasions, Toni was hospitalized. Nothing seemed to be helping. Toni was lost, hopeless, and deeply depressed.

On one of her mother's many trips to Texas, she suggested that she take Toni home with her. Her mom thought that maybe it would snap her out of her depression. After all, not being able to get out of bed and seeing her family and her kids falling apart were making things worse for Toni. Her mom suggested that we get her out of Texas and get her some R & R for three or four weeks to see if that helped. Though I didn't want to see Toni leave, it felt like a relief for me since there would be one less person for me to take care of.

So, Toni went to New York with her parents. While she was gone, a group of people from church fasted and prayed for Toni's recovery. By this time, things were getting really rough for me. My life felt like a juggling act with my concern for Toni, taking care of the children and the home, and leading our growing youth ministry. But my family was my priority. Since I wasn't sure I could continue doing all I was responsible for, I began to seriously consider taking a temporary leave of absence from youth ministry in order to take care of my family. About the time I was having these thoughts, I received an invitation from the church in San Diego to speak at the youth groups' Graduation Banquet. Most of the graduates had been in my youth ministry, and I knew and loved them. However, with all that I was dealing with, I was ready to respectfully decline their offer. However, I had a second thought. If I could go to San Diego and get away from everything and everyone to be with God, maybe He would speak to me and give me direction as to what I should do.

I called Skyline Church in San Diego and told them that I would be their Graduation Banquet speaker if they would allow me an extra day to spend time alone with God. They happily agreed, and I was off to San Diego in search of answers from Heaven. I told the Lord that though I was going to speak to the graduates, I was really going to San Diego because I needed to hear from Him.

There had been times during Toni's illness when I sat in the living room late at night and asked God why He was allowing Toni and my family to suffer so terribly. I was so frustrated that I cried out to God on a number of occasions asking Him to, "Step in! Step in and do something! Why are you allowing this to happen to me?"

I wasn't so much questioning God, but I just couldn't understand why He was allowing this. After all, I was His child, His servant! I felt so helpless. One of my coping mechanisms was to work on my home. Although I'm not a finish carpenter, I added crown molding and changed out the floor moldings and door casings in every room of my home. The hammering was a great way to release frustration. Besides, it was one of the few things in my life that I felt I could control. One thing was for sure, I couldn't control what my wife was going through. I guess I just didn't realize that I was in the School of Brokenness, and God was using suffering to mold me into the man He wanted me to be.

I flew to California on a Sunday afternoon to speak at the evening Grad Banquet. It was a formal banquet so, reluctantly, I had brought a suit with me. However, upon arriving in San Diego I discovered that my luggage had not arrived. I would not be able to wear my suit…and I was thrilled! Students attending the banquet were decked out in tuxedos and gowns, but I attended in a pair of shorts and a T-shirt. It was awesome! Believe it or not, God was working behind the scenes in allowing my luggage to be lost. (I'll have more on that later.) After speaking at the banquet I returned to my hotel with great anticipation. I planned to meet with God the next day.

I did not have a chance to spend time reading the Bible that night since I was still without my luggage, and my Bible was packed in it. I went to sleep praying, "Lord, tomorrow is a day I have set aside for You. Please give me direction because I really don't know what to do."

Early the next morning, I left the hotel and walked to a place called Mt. Helix to begin an intense Prayer Walk. Mt. Helix is a well-known place in San Diego primarily because it has a big cross at its top. I had to walk under Highway 8 on my way to Mt. Helix, and I was so focused that I didn't keep track of where the hotel was located. I started up Mt. Helix and eventually came to an elevated surface overlooking the area. I looked back towards Highway 8 and saw my hotel, Grossmont High School, and Grossmont Junior College with the beautiful mountains of Southern California in the background. It seemed like I was able to see most of San Diego County from this spot. At this point, it seemed that the Lord spoke to me,

"Joe," he said, "Just as you feel like you are seeing all of San Diego County, I see all of your life. Before you got to this elevated place your view was very limited. Now that you are at a higher place, you have a much better view, and you can see so much more. Joe, I see everything, and I want you to know that when you're in a state of confusion and you don't understand things that are happening, don't believe for a moment that I don't know what's going on. I want you to know that you can trust Me."

A great blanket of comfort seemed to enfold me. I was lovingly reminded that from God's viewpoint, He sees everything in my life, and He is still in control.

It was one of those California days when it was fifty degrees in the morning heading to ninety-five in the afternoon. I imagined the cross as the destination where I would meet Jesus, and I was not going to stop until I got to that cross. The climb was steep and winding. At times, I lost sight of the cross. I questioned whether I was still on Mt. Helix, or if I was on a different mountain that bordered it. At times, I could not see the cross.

I sensed the Lord saying, "Keep walking."

I wanted to stop, to go back down and make sure I was on the right mountain, but again I sensed the Lord saying, "Keep walking." So I kept walking. Then suddenly the cross appeared, and because I was closer to it this time, I could see it more clearly.

I continued my walk. For a time I would see the cross, and then for a time I would lose sight of the cross. One time the cross disappeared from my sight for what seemed like more than ten minutes. "Where is the cross?" I wondered. But as I continued up the trail, there—right before my eyes—was the cross again, this time with the sun shining upon it. It looked almost as if it were glowing with the glory of God. In this amazing moment, the Lord said

"Joe, often times when things get tough, you will feel like you are climbing a mountain. There will be times you will find it difficult to continue, and times that you will not be able to see Me. But keep on climbing and walking by faith, even when you can't see Me. If you keep climbing in these types of situations, I will appear to you and you will see Me more clearly than you have ever seen Me before. Just like the cross is more radiant with the sun shining upon it, you will see Me more radiantly when you learn to keep walking by faith through the tough times."

Wow! This Prayer Walk had exceeded my expectations. The peace of God filled my heart as I continued walking, feeling as if I were on a journey with the Lord.

Finally I reached the cross, and it was awesome. There in the midst of the beautiful mountains of San Diego, the Lord gently spoke to me.

"Joe, I will soon restore Toni. I'm going to restore her, and she is going to be okay. You will not have to take a break from youth ministry. Just relax and trust Me."

Even though Toni was still at her parent's home in New York, to me it was as if she was already home and healed. Though Toni had been sick for nearly nine months and we had tried just about everything to help her get better, in that moment I knew the healing work was done.

At this point in my Prayer Walk, I was kind of floating in the Lord's presence. A couple of hours had passed before I realized that I had no idea where I was. I have a terrible sense of direction and seem to get lost pretty often. However, I had complete confidence that the Lord was guiding me. There would be no getting lost on this day.

The Lord spoke to me again. He said, "Since you came all the way out to San Diego to meet with Me, I am going to lay out for you the rest of your life in ministry."

And He did just that!

"Joe, some day you are going to plant a church."

Now I had worked as a youth pastor in three different churches, all considered mega-churches. The youth group I was presently leading had over 500 students in it.

But God said, "The church you plant will be smaller, but it will be very fruitful."

What an awesome word from the Lord. Needless to say, this Prayer Walk was one of the greatest experiences of my life.

About this time I found myself in the town of La Mesa, pretty much lost. I didn't have a clue where my hotel was, but I didn't worry for a second. I knew that God was leading me and that He was going to take me right back to my hotel—wherever that might be. I kept walking. I turned around a bend, and there was my hotel. I walked into the lobby and made my way to the front desk.

I was pretty sweaty from this two-and-a-half hour prayer walk, but I felt as spiritually refreshed as one can feel. The person at the front desk called out to me that my luggage had arrived. I thanked him and picked up my luggage. Once I was in the room, the Lord again spoke to my heart.

"Joe, now I want to speak to you from My Word."

I opened my luggage and pulled out my Bible. I had been on a plan to read through the entire Bible, and I felt led to pick up where I had left off. I opened my Bible to the bookmark in II Chronicles Chapter 1. If the airline had not lost my luggage, I would not have been up to II Chronicles Chapter 1, because I would have read that chapter the night before. The loss of my luggage was the reason I was about to read this particular passage of scripture. It told of a dream in which God had appeared to Solomon shortly after he had been anointed King of Israel.

That night God appeared to Solomon and said to him, "Ask for whatever you want me to give you." Solomon answered God, "You have shown great kindness to David my father and have made me king in his place. Now, Lord God, let your promise to my father David be confirmed, for you have made me king over a people who are as numerous as the dust of the earth. Give me wisdom and knowledge, that I may lead this people, for who is able to govern this great people of yours?"

In II Chronicles 1:7-10, having made Solomon King of Israel, God was giving Solomon the opportunity to ask for anything. Solomon could have asked for military dominance over the world. He could have asked for financial blessings. He could have asked for a wonderful woman. Though Solomon didn't always make wise choices, at this point in his life, he was spot-on. He asked God to give him wisdom and knowledge so that he could lead these people well. As I read this scripture, I sensed the Lord saying to me,

"Joe, I've just laid out the rest of your life in ministry. Now Joe, what do you want me to give you so you will be able to fulfill what I have called you to do?"

What an encounter! What a moment! My answer was, "Lord, I want you to be able to accomplish your will through me."

And the Lord said to my heart, "Your request is granted."

Let me tell you what my day with God accomplished in my life:

First, I was spiritually renewed. Before the trip I had felt worn out, but I wasn't worn out any more. I think I could have run all the way home from San Diego—"Forest Gump" style. I was renewed because God had touched my heart.

Second, I knew God was about to do a healing work in Toni's life. I remember talking to Toni on the phone in New York after my trip to San Diego. She said, "I don't understand what's happening, but the clouds are clearing up. I'm starting to think straight again."

When I picked Toni up at the airport just three weeks later, she was smiling with that beautiful smile of hers. It seemed like I hadn't seen her smile in nine months, but she was back and restored.

Third, I now clearly knew my next step in ministry, though it would be years down the road.

And fourth, I had a brand new anointing on my life and ministry. God would use me to bring about His will through my life. With this new anointing, I would soon become a leader of leaders among youth pastors in the DFW area.

I was so grateful to God for meeting me in such a significant way. I had survived my first semester in the School of Brokenness, and I was all the better as a result of this training.

Chapter Twenty-One

Hot Tub Prayer

My mother was diagnosed with breast cancer in 1982. I was with her when the doctor diagnosed her cancer. In fact, I was the one the doctor privately told that she only had 6 months to live. Thankfully, my mom lived for another 12 years after that diagnosis.

During that time, I had the opportunity to lead her to Christ. Her cancer was instrumental in her coming to Christ. The reality of death has a way of making a person think about eternal things, and it was truly a blessing to be the one to lead my mother to trust Christ as her Savior.

After my mom died, my dad was left alone in their big house in Brooklyn. Although he had had a stroke, he was fully recovered and in good health. I tried to get to New York on a semi-annual basis to visit with him and to make sure he was doing all right. On one such visit we went out to dinner. I was surprised when he unexpectedly asked me if he could move in with my family. He said he was tired of living alone and was hoping he could move to Texas to stay with my family for the remainder of his life. I told him that I needed to talk it over with Toni first and then would get back to him.

When I got home I told Toni about my dad's request. She immediately said, "Yes, of course he can." We talked to the children, also, and they agreed it would be a good thing to do. Then I called my dad and gave him the good news.

Now, my dad was never one who liked hot weather. Have you ever been to Texas in the summer? It takes hot to a new level. For that reason, I suggested that he come out and visit Texas and experience the climate before deciding to move in with us. He did come to Texas, and he stayed with us for a week. To my surprise, he loved it! He decided that once he closed things out in Brooklyn, he would indeed move in with us. What he said next really took me by surprise. He wanted us to sell our house and buy a bigger and better house where he could have his own separate living quarters. He handed me a very large check and told me to put the money towards the new house. When I looked at the check, I was shocked. I had never seen a check for that much money.

"Dad, you don't have to give us that money."

"I want you to buy a bigger house and build me my own apartment in that house. Take the money," he said. "When you have the house and my quarters are completed, I will move to Texas."

I took the check to the bank to deposit it. When I handed the check to the teller, he looked at the amount and said, "Holy Moly!" I had to smile.

Our house sold not long after we put it on the market.

We found another home that was bigger and better. We moved in, and I began making plans to build my dad his own apartment. After a couple of months of work, his living quarters were completed. Our house was ready for my dad to move in, but his move to Texas was being delayed. He was having a hard time selling his home in Brooklyn.

During this time, my dad called me and said, "Joe, would you like to have a pool at the new house?"

"Dad, I can't afford a pool!"

"I didn't ask you if you can afford a pool; I asked you if you would like to have a pool," he said.

"Well, I think we'd all love to have a pool but…."

He said, "Go and have a pool built. I will pay for it."

I said, "Dad, you don't have to…."

He stopped me in mid-sentence and said, "Listen, Joe, you're making this difficult. Find out how much it will cost to build a pool, and I will pay for it."

Well, thanks to my dad, we now had a big, beautiful house with a big beautiful yard, a beautiful apartment for my dad, and a beautiful pool with a hot tub!

I had been taking Prayer Walks every day for quite some time. I did a lot of talking to God, and it was great. But, as I began to use my hot tub, I found it also to be a great place to pray. I found that I could not only talk to God when praying in the hot tub, but I would also listen. I began to learn the art of listening to God. As a result, the hot tub quickly replaced Prayer Walking as my main place of connecting with God. The times I spent in the hot tub would become invaluable to me as I continued my course work in the School of Brokenness.

When a person pursues a relationship with God over the years, he or she accumulates a collection of experiences. If that person is paying attention, he or she will begin to recognize patterns of how God works in their lives. This type of history is invaluable in times of confusion. When tough times come, it is a source of comfort to lean on those past experiences/encounters with God as a pattern of God's faithfulness. I would need that history very soon.

At this time, the youth ministry at Pantego Bible Church had developed beyond my wildest dreams. We had hundreds of students participating in our youth ministry. Many of their parents and families were now coming to the church as well. We had grown from a small youth group into a huge youth ministry. I had three full-time youth pastors on my staff, in addition to 15 Bible College and Seminary Interns. The church was flourishing as a result of the youth ministry's success. Though I had worked hard to help us get to where we were, I knew that it was God who was causing the success of our ministry. I attributed much of what we were accomplishing to the time I was spending prayer walking and praying in the hot tub. God was meeting me when I prayed, guiding and directing much of what we were doing. Though many were giving me the credit for what was being accomplished, I knew that God was the One responsible for our success. These were my greatest days in youth ministry. I was happy and fulfilled doing youth ministry at this church.

Pantego Bible Church was in a relocation process. They wanted to move the church to another location with the hope that they would become a regional mega-church. However, the relocation of Pantego Bible Church brought with it some great disappointments and some great challenges to the church, and more specifically, to me.

The two previous churches that I had worked at had also been in the process of relocating. However, I didn't make it to the new locations at either of the previous churches. But, I did make it to the new location at Pantego. Because of the way the church handled the relocation, just one month after moving to the "promised land," I was angry, disillusioned, and burned out. The church used poor judgment and made so many bad decisions that I abruptly resigned from my position as youth pastor. This became another one of those defining moments for me. This had to be getting a little old for Toni.

After I resigned, I began to question whether the 17 years I had spent working in church had been well spent. I was walking away feeling as if my time spent had been wasted. It was a period of assessment for me. It was also a period of confusion and disillusion. The church graciously gave me a two-month sabbatical over the summer hoping I would reconsider my decision to resign. I believed that the relocation was not handled in a way that honored God, and I did not feel I could support the vision of this church any longer.

I entered the summer of 2001 with a lot of questions about the way churches functioned. I also entered that summer with a lot of time to think. I was in a season of brokenness, which should not have come as a surprise since I was still enrolled in the School of Brokenness. The good news was that I still had my hot tub as a place to talk to and listen to God.

If I had entered this latest season of suffering during the time I was having my Word of Life-style quiet times, lying in bed falling in and out of sleep, I don't think I would have survived. I could easily have ended up as a spiritual casualty. But, because I had found a way to significantly connect with God, I was prepared to face the challenges that I faced in life and ministry. In this time of confusion, my history with God would serve me well, and would provide the basis to carry me through.

Chapter Twenty-Two

Divine Pruning

My father's decision to pay for a pool and hot tub at our home turned out to be a greater gift than I could ever have expected. Many of the things that God was going to teach me would be taught during my times with Him in my hot tub.

I had begun my unplanned summer sabbatical after angrily resigning from my church position. Although I was outraged, I think I was more disillusioned and hurt. I had trusted the people I served with in ministry to operate with integrity, but the actions I had witnessed did not demonstrate integrity. I was very disappointed in the way the church had handled the relocation, and I began to think that maybe I was finished working in the church. Though this affected my view of the church, it had no effect on my relationship with God. Thankfully, I had always made the distinction between God and the church; so even in this difficult time, my relationship with God was alive and well—even thriving!

When I stepped down from my position as youth pastor, it created a sense of excitement among some of my friends. Their excitement was based on the thought that I would soon start a church. Nothing could have been further from the truth—I was in no way considering leadership in the church anymore. I didn't even want to attend church. I experienced some pressure from a few of my friends, but it was my wife, Toni, who was putting the most pressure on me.

She constantly asked, "Joe, why don't you plant a church?"

And I constantly answered, "I don't want to plant a church!"

We went back and forth so many times that I began to ask her if she wanted to plant a church. Even though God had made it clear to me on the Prayer Walk on Mt. Helix that someday I would indeed plant a church, at this particular time in my life I could not imagine taking that step of faith. I was disillusioned. I was hurt. I was angry. And, I needed time to heal.

I came to realize through this situation that when we are down, it is very easy to forget the things that God has called us to do. Only a few years earlier, before my life-changing prayer walk on Mt. Helix, my wife had been sick and I had been considering stepping out of ministry for a while to care for my family. On that prayer walk in San Diego, God had met with me in a powerful way to tell me He was going to restore my wife, that she would be okay, and that I did not need to step out of ministry. Then God showed me that when the going gets rough and it seems I can't see Him, I need to keep walking. As I walk by faith I will see Him more clearly than ever before. And then the Lord showed me the rest of my life in ministry. And what did he tell me he was going to do through me? I was going to plant a church. Now, here I am just a few years later, disillusioned and hurt, having forgotten most of what God had told me!

When I said I wasn't going to plant a church, I wasn't being disobedient to God. I had just forgotten what He said. I needed to be reminded of my calling.

Abraham, also known as the Father of our faith, was called by God when he was 75 years old. God promised to give him and his wife Sarah a son, a great nation, and a land. When God fulfilled these promises, Abraham and Sarah had a son named Isaac, they parented a nation called Israel, and the land of Canaan became theirs. Abraham's entire life was based on these promises, particularly the promise that he and Sarah would have a son.

Twenty-four years after God made that promise, Sarah had still not become pregnant, and Abraham still did not have the son that had been promised. Then, God appeared again to Abraham when he was 99 years old (Genesis 17) and confirmed that he and Sarah would indeed have a son. Abraham simply laughed, demonstrating that he no longer believed that this promise would come to pass. The passing of time had convinced Abraham that God's promise would not be fulfilled. Sarah had a similar reaction (Genesis 18), demonstrating that she, also, no longer believed that this promise would come to pass.

Now, Abraham is known as the Father of our faith, and here we see him doubting the very promise God had made to him. Abraham needed to be reminded of God's promise. If a great man of faith like Abraham, needed to be reminded of God's promise, then I guess it was okay if I needed to be reminded, also.

There are many reasons we as Christians attend church: to worship God with other believers, to learn the Word of God, to fellowship, to be encouraged, and to take communion together. But I also believe we come to church to be reminded. Though occasionally we might hear something that we have never heard before, for the most part sermons remind us of truths that we already know. When we stop going to church, it becomes very easy to forget incidences of God's mercy and grace. When we forget details about the Lord's work in our lives, we become spiritually vulnerable and it becomes easy for us to fall away from our faith. It is vital for us to be reminded.

I was in a very vulnerable place at this time. It would have been easy for me to fall away. I needed God to remind me of some of the promises He had emphatically spoken into my life which I seemed to have forgotten.

I was on my unplanned summer sabbatical when God

began to work on me. I questioned whether my involvement in church over the past 17 years had been worth the investment. About this time, I stumbled across a book called, *Fresh Wind, Fresh Fire,* by Jim Cymbala. Jim is the pastor of Brooklyn Tabernacle Church, an incredible church located in the heart of Brooklyn that is attended by thousands. Brooklyn Tabernacle has a great ministry that reaches people from all walks of life. They minister to prostitutes, drug addicts, and the homeless, as well as to mainstream people. I began reading the story about how God called Jim to plant this church in Brooklyn. From the very beginning, Pastor Cymbala determined to keep the main thing as the main thing: loving God and reaching people. As I read this book, one chapter each day, I saw how God was using that church to change lives. It was especially meaningful to me because I was reading about a man who was doing church in the way I believed it was supposed to be done. This was a way of doing church that was worth giving one's life to. As disillusioned as I was about the church, this book was giving me hope. It was renewing and refreshing me.

I was also spending a lot of time in my hot tub, praying and listening to God. My yard was large and beautifully landscaped, but against the side fence some red tip photinias were growing wild and out of control. I looked at these shrubs in desperate need of attention, and my landscaping passion kicked in. I decided to trim the photinias. When I began trimming the shrubs, I realized they were not even in my yard, but were in my neighbor's yard. I had to climb over my neighbor's fence to prune this overgrown shrub. By the time I finished my project, there was little left of the shrub. It looked like all the life was taken out of it. Honestly, it looked like a skeleton. Though it was the middle of summer, all of the leaves were gone. I figured the leaves would grow back soon enough, but at least I had tamed this wild shrub.

Later that night, I was in the hot tub staring at my work project of the day. Suddenly, I felt a strange connection with the recently pruned photinia. Just as the life appeared to be taken out of this once healthy shrub, so it felt that all the ministry life had been taken out of me.

That was when the Lord seemed to whisper in my ear, "Joe, you feel this way because I have been pruning you."

That took me by surprise because I was sure that I was a victim, caught in the unfortunate crossfire of a church that had gotten sidetracked from the main thing: loving God and ministering to people. My church had gotten caught up in the building game, and I felt like I was one of its casualties. However, the soft voice of God was revealing my circumstances to be much different. A scripture I had memorized long ago slipped silently into my consciousness. Jesus is speaking:

I am the true vine and my Father is the gardener. He cuts off every branch in me that bears no fruit while every branch that does bear fruit he prunes so that it will be even more fruitful.

– John 15:1-2

Then I sensed God saying to me: "Joe, I am pruning you, and when you experience pruning in your life, it is painful. But it will result in your bearing more fruit."

Those words ministered deeply to my heart. Could it be that God was using this situation in my life to make me better and even more fruitful? That would sure make sense of all of this!

Over the next few weeks, I began to notice new leaves sprouting from the once hacked-up photinia. Was it possible that new life was about to begin sprouting in my life? Only time would tell.

Chapter Twenty-Three

The Call to Plant a Church

I was gradually being renewed and restored during my summer sabbatical. I was still not feeling the desire to attend church, but for the sake of our children, Toni and I decided it was time for us to attend a local church in Arlington while we waited for the Lord to give us clear direction. The church we visited was somewhat traditional and not really the style we were used to or preferred, but it was close to home and the pastor was a good friend of mine. After we had attended a few times, Toni and I got involved in a Sunday School class, but I realized from my experience in this church that I would never be comfortable in this type of environment.

During this time I got a call from a church that had learned I was not currently doing ministry. It was a very large, prestigious church located in Dallas. They said they were looking for a college pastor and wondered if I would be interested. I didn't really know if I was interested or not. At my wife's urging, I went through a couple of interviews. The staff seemed to like my ideas, my vision, and my passion. They offered me the job. They were willing to let me continue living in Arlington and commute to the church. Their focus was in bringing change to the church by moving to a more modern approach to ministry. Aware of the challenge of change, they hoped I could introduce some of my ideas, and hopefully, people would catch on. It seemed risky to me. I thought about the possibility of working at this church, but I didn't have peace. I did not want to go where I didn't fully embrace what the church was doing. I didn't think risking another bad church experience would be wise. I graciously turned them down.

My wife was not exactly excited with my decision, but she was still supportive. The amazing thing to me was that even though God had clearly called me to plant a church, I still seemed to have forgotten. However, God was actually beginning to warm my heart to the thought that just maybe, I would plant a church.

Though I no longer worked at Pantego Bible Church, I was consulting with the pastor and trying to help with the transition of the youth ministry. Since I had left abruptly, the youth ministry was not doing very well. I was trying to be available to help. I had an afternoon meeting with the pastor, and we spent time talking about the youth ministry. Then, he asked me a question: "Joe, what are you going to do? What is your next step?"

I told him I was not really sure. Then I said, "I think I might plant a church."

He looked me in the eye and said, "I think that you will be an awesome church planter."

When he spoke those words, it deeply touched my heart. When you work for someone for seven years and they tell you they really believe you can do something, it is very encouraging.

As I drove home after that meeting, I told the Lord, "Maybe I will plant a church. Lord, if you want me to plant a church, show me. Show me you want me to take this step, and I will do it."

I got home about 3:30 p.m. after having just prayed a serious prayer asking God to confirm if He wanted me to plant a church. God was working on my behalf to make sure that I did not miss His answer.

About 4:30 p.m., the phone rang. It was a woman named DuAnn. She and I had worked together in San Diego at Skyline Church. DuAnn had a thick Southern accent and had recently moved back to her home state of Alabama. She asked if I was still doing youth ministry. I said no and told her I was between jobs, and I was not really sure about my next step. Then DuAnn got to the point of the call. She and her husband lived in Madison, Alabama, and there wasn't a Wesleyan Church in their community. They wanted to take steps to start one. She explained that she and Todd had met with Wesleyan denominational leaders and had presented their request to have a church planted in Madison.

By this time, I realized that something divine was

taking place. She said that the denominational leaders had approved their request, and they were now searching for someone to be the planter. DuAnn said that I was the first one they thought of for this position.

Then DuAnn asked, "Joe, would you consider coming to Madison, Alabama, to plant a church?"

One hour after I had asked God to show me if He wanted me to plant a church, I got this phone call. Wow! I was gasping for air.

I said, "DuAnn, get your husband Todd on the phone!"

I explained the series of events leading to her phone call, and then they were gasping for air.

She called the Wesleyan denomination leaders, and that afternoon we had a conference call.

None of us could believe how clearly God had answered my prayer. I was now forever convinced that God had called me to plant a church. The people in Alabama wanted me to come out for an interview as soon as possible. For them, it was merely a formality. I agreed to come and go through the interview process. I hung up the phone, astonished at how clearly God had met me and answered my prayer.

When Toni came home from work that evening, I pulled her aside and said, "Honey, we're planting a church."

She celebrated until I told her it might be in Alabama. Then she had a "deer-in-the-headlights" look. However, we both knew that God would make the location for the church plant clear. We rejoiced that I knew my next step in ministry.

Bobby was a friend who I had met years before while I was youth pastor in Staten Island. He had a very rough upbringing in Staten Island: deep involvement in drugs, alcohol, and violence. He had visited our church and I was able to lead him to Christ. Bobby had become a youth pastor in California and then in Kansas. Recently, he and wife Heidi had moved to Texas, and he was with me through the rough times at Pantego. He planned to help me with the planting of the church, so I decided to take Bobby with me to Alabama to pursue this call.

First, we went to Tuscaloosa to meet with the denominational leaders. I was getting a little nervous because Bobby was a New Yorker through and through. (If you remember the character that Joe Pesci played in "My Cousin Vinnie," including the NY accent, then you get an idea of my friend Bobby.) We were driving through Mississippi and stopped for gas and food. I asked Bobby not to talk to ensure our safety.

We arrived in Tuscaloosa and met with the Wesleyan leaders; then we drove north to Madison to meet with Todd and DuAnn. The Wesleyans wanted us to plant the church. They offered a full two-years of salary to help get the plant off the ground. Todd and DuAnn also wanted

189

us to plant the church. They thought I would make a great planter in the Madison area. But, did God want us to plant this church in Alabama? I had an uneasy feeling about the Deep South. I had noticed confederate flags on pickup trucks and hanging in front of some stores. The red dirt freaked me out a little, as well. Alabama did not seem to be a likely place for a Yankee. I can't explain it, but I just wasn't feeling it in Alabama.

On the drive home, with the offer officially before us, I asked Bobby what he thought. He said, "Joe, this is your call. I'll go with you, but you make the decision."

When we stopped for food, I called Toni. I said, "We had a great time, but I don't think Alabama is the place for our family."

Toni rejoiced, and I knew that the door had closed in Madison.

Bobby and I began to think: Why not just start a church in Arlington? I knew so many people in this city; we already lived there; we both loved the place. It was my home—so why not start a church in Arlington?

Bobby agreed. On the ride home we came up with the name for the church—"Crossroads." We decided to start the church in the living room of my home. I was so excited that God had clearly called me to plant a church and that it would be in Arlington, Texas.

One evening shortly after arriving home from the trip

to Alabama, I was spending time in the hot tub, and I noticed that there was life on those photinias. The leaves had come back completely, and the plant was healthier than ever, thanks to the great pruning job I had done. And God said, "When I prune you, you become stronger, healthier, and better." And that is exactly what happened to me. I didn't enjoy the pruning—it hurt as I was going through it—but the result of the pruning was a healthy tree full of new life. I couldn't wait to begin the church.

However, there were more lessons to be learned, more pruning to be done, and more suffering to endure.

Chapter Twenty-Four

From Arlington, to Staten Island, to New Jersey

I was excited to be planting a church in Arlington, Texas. It was going to be a different kind of church than the ones I had previously served in. It would be a church worth giving my life to. I started spreading the word. The church was to start in my house. People were getting excited.

I met with a pastor friend of mine from another church in the city. Gary recommended that before I started this church in Arlington that I ask Pantego Bible Church for their blessing. It sounded like a reasonable request. I told Gary I would pray about it. That night in the hot tub I set up a way for God to confirm that He wanted me to plant the church in Arlington. I said, "Lord, if it is Your will that I plant this church here and now in Arlington, then let Pantego Bible Church give me their blessing. If they won't give me their blessing, then I won't plant the church in Arlington. To be honest, I never thought there was even a remote possibility that I wouldn't receive their blessing to plant this church.

I met with the elders at Pantego. I was excited. I told them what I felt God calling me to do. Then I asked for their blessing to start the church. I was a little surprised when they said they wanted to think about it. I told them I would give them time to think it over and call them back. I called back about a week later. They said they still hadn't made their decision. Now I was a little nervous. What decision had to be made? I wasn't asking for financial support, just for their blessing to plant a church.

Three weeks later, the first week of September, one of the elders called me with their answer. He said they wouldn't give me their blessing to plant a church in Arlington. I went silent on the phone.

Shocked, I said, "What did you say?"

He repeated, "We won't give you our blessing to plant a church. We want you to wait one year before starting a church in Arlington."

Surprised by their answer, I began to reason as to why they would not want me to plant a church there. Pantego Bible Church had recently moved into a new and expensive building. Because of their poor decisions, people were leaving the church. They were concerned that if I started a church they might lose more people. That would create some real financial problems.

Looking back, I know that God's sovereign hand was guiding their decision. I'm not saying it was a good decision. But, I was in the School of Brokenness, and God had lessons for me to learn. He used these things to help me become the man He wanted me to be.

Pantego Bible Church had said no, and I was devastated. I was already dealing with anger and disillusionment from the poorly handled relocation process, and I had just begun to recover from that. It was the first week in September, 2001. Four days after I received their refusal to give their blessing, the attack on the World Trade Center took place. When I was growing up, I could look out of my parent's bedroom window and see the Twin Towers. Now, they were forever gone. My friends and family in New York were suffering terribly. Even though I had been out of New York for 10 years, I felt a renewed allegiance to my home. In the aftermath of 9/11, I knew I had to make a visit to New York. My wife supported my desire to go to New York, so I began the 24-hour drive solo.

I was driving on Interstate 30 just east of Dallas when the Spirit of God came upon me like it had never come upon me before. God began to show me that He was not calling me to start a church in Arlington, but He was calling me to go back to New York City and plant a church there. The Spirit of God came on me so heavily that I cried uncontrollably from Dallas through most of Arkansas. Everything began to make sense to me. God was calling me to go back to reach my people in their greatest moment of need.

I stopped overnight in Tennessee and called Toni. I said, "Honey, God is calling me to plant a church in New

York City. He's calling us home!"

Toni began to cry and said that was where she wanted to go. She said, "Let's go home and reach our people."

The next day I drove the rest of the way to New York City. The first person I met with was the pastor of the church I used to work at in Staten Island. We went to a Diner for lunch. I told him about the incredible call of God on my life to plant a church and to come back to New York. I told him I was excited at the thought of working in the city beside my former pastor—the man who was responsible for leading me to Christ.

There were 750,000 people living in Staten Island, and this was the place I believed God was calling me. I told the pastor that I was excited about working together, about being fellow pastors, about being ministry partners.

He looked across the table and said, "You can't plant a church in Staten Island."

"What do you mean I can't plant a church in Staten Island? What are you talking about?" I asked. "Remember the phone call from Alabama? The drive on Interstate 30—crying from Texas to Arkansas? I believe that God has called me to plant a church in Staten Island!"

He explained that since I left New York City from his church, I would have to come back to New York City through his church. He said if I wanted his blessing to come back to New York City, I would have to come back to his church, work for one or two years on their staff, and if or when they thought I was ready, they would send me somewhere in New York City, at their discretion, to plant a church.

Here I was again, facing resistance from the very one I expected to support me. Once again I was becoming angry and feeling disillusioned.

I left lunch that day with a burning pain in the pit of my stomach. I just couldn't understand why my interaction with church leaders was so difficult. I went to the home of a friend named Willie. I was distraught, angry, disillusioned, devastated—you name it; I felt it. I stayed at Willie's for nine hours trying to make sense of the roadblocks I kept hitting. Though I didn't believe there was any biblical foundation for what this pastor was asking me to do, I decided I would not fight him. I would not go back and work at that church, but neither would I start a church in Staten Island.

I left Willie's home and traveled across the Outerbridge Crossing to New Jersey where I would stay with my brother Bob and his family. It was during my stay at his house that I had the opportunity to lead his wife Joyce to faith in Christ. I told my brother about the meeting with the pastor and the roadblock he was putting up. My brother and sister-in-law told me to forget Staten Island. They invited me to plant a church right there in

Monmouth County, New Jersey. They said I could help them reach their friends. I pondered their suggestion. It seemed to make sense.

I called Toni, and again my supportive wife was there for me. She agreed with this slightly adjusted plan. The church plant location was set—Monmouth County, New Jersey. Monmouth County is a bedroom community of New York City. Nearly all of the people who live in that area work in New York City. In fact, the highest concentration of people who died in the Towers on 9/11 were residents of Monmouth County. This would be the place I would plant the church.

When I returned from my trip to New York, reality set in. I was moving to New Jersey, the Garden State. I began to develop a plan. The primary issue that would determine when we moved would be raising the necessary finances. I contacted church denominations and was excited to find three different denominations willing to partner with me on the church plant. The Christian and Missionary Alliance, the Wesleyans, and the Southern Baptists all approved me as a church planter. I was very encouraged. In addition, many families of students from my former youth ministry also wanted to financially support me. Things began to fall into place.

Toni and I decided to place our home on the market to be sold. I contacted my real estate agent and she prepared a contract. I was about to sign it when she realized that she also needed Toni's signature. I considered driving to the school where Toni worked as a school nurse to get her signature, but I decided to take the contract home and let her sign it that night. I would take it to the real estate agent the next day.

That night, I received a call from a man who had heard that we were going to move. He was interested in the house and wanted to look at it. He came that same night, looked it over, and said he would take it. I tore up the agent's unsigned contract, amazed how God had worked so quickly and had also saved me the 6 percent real estate fee!

The buyer had one stipulation to this quick sale. He wanted to move into the house in eleven days. We signed the deal, but we didn't have a home to move into. I made a couple of phone calls, and within 24 hours, located a rental house only 3 blocks from my home. It was owned by a friend. Although it didn't have a separate apartment for my dad, it did have two master bedrooms. Eleven days later we moved out of our house.

After moving our furniture into our new rental house, I told Toni I had to go back to the old house and finish some business. I needed to meet with God one more time in the hot tub. It was the place that God brought about such great change in my life. He had allowed me to be pruned, and in doing so had changed the way I viewed church. I wanted to meet Him there one more time. I stayed in the hot tub that night for 3 hours. My skin was wrinkled and I was dehydrated, but God filled my spirit. I cherished every minute of our last time together in that special place.

Towards the end of the three hours, the Lord spoke to my heart. There was a full moon that night, and I sensed the Lord saying to me: "You see the moon clearly because you had laser surgery on your eyes."

Had I not undergone laser eye surgery, I would not have been able to distinguish more than just a bright light in the sky. The laser surgery enabled me to see the full moon clearly that night.

Then the Lord spoke these words: "Joe, in these past few months I have done laser surgery on your heart. Now you see more clearly what I want in a church. Take what I have taught you and go plant a church that is worth giving your life to. Don't ever forget what I have taught you."

In this special moment, in this special place, God once again touched my heart as only He can. I had learned and changed so much. Now, I was ready to put these things into practice.

When you learn something the hard way, it tends to go deep into the heart. The things God had been teaching me had done a transforming work in my life. This School of Brokenness, though difficult, was reaping great rewards for me.

When I got out of that hot tub for the last time, I knew my job was to find a home in New Jersey, move my family, and begin what I believed would be my life's work: the planting of Crossroads Community Church in Monmouth County, New Jersey. However, I was not ready to graduate from the School of Brokenness just yet. God still had to deal with some other things in my life. He wasn't pleased about the way I had become so angry at the church, and also with my great difficulty in letting go of my anger. My loving heavenly Father intended to deal with me.

Years later, the church leadership of Pantego Bible Church apologized for not giving us their full blessing. Pantego Bible Church is a wonderful church, and their Senior Pastor, David, is a good friend of mine to this day.

Chapter Twenty-Five

Scheming to Live Large in New Jersey

It was time to get to work planting a church. God had clearly called me to plant a church, and I now knew it was to be in New Jersey. I began traveling there on a regular basis. I stayed with my brother when I was there, but I needed to find a home for our family. I also needed to develop relationships with people who would help me start the church.

The ironic part of my going back to the New York City area to plant a church was that deep down, I had always believed that God would call me back there. Because I had fallen in love with Arlington, I often said, "I'm never going back to New York," or "I hate New York City." Often, I told friends, "If you ever hear me say that I'm going to New York, you will know that idea had to come from God because I don't want anything to do with that place. If it's up to me, I will never go back there." Though I said those things half-joking, a part of me was serious. I did not want to leave Texas. I loved the hot weather; I loved how everything is so spread out and large; and I loved the people. There wasn't anything about Texas that I did not love. Every time I spoke negatively about New York, I got a prodding that I was despising God's future call on my life.

Now I knew that I had despised God's call, for His intent was to indeed send me back home. I was grateful that God let me off easy on that one.

I found a real estate agent in New Jersey named Amy. Although we had gotten a great price for our home in Texas, New Jersey house prices were much higher, and I was prepared to spend more on a house there than I had spent in Texas. I gave Amy my price range, and we began looking at homes. I knew things would be a lot more expensive in New Jersey, but I was shocked at just how much more expensive a comparable house in New Jersey would be. I didn't realize that I had gotten used to living large in Texas. The house my father helped me purchase was a 4,000 square foot custom home—by far the nicest and largest home I had ever lived in. A house like it in New Jersey could cost well over a million dollars, quite a bit more than I had gotten when I sold my home in Texas.

We began to look at homes in New Jersey that were within my price range, but I soon became very discouraged. One particular Saturday while looking at homes, I remember thinking, "I am not going back to living that way." At that moment, I sensed a prodding from the Lord concerning that ugly thought. When I first became a Christian, I had the willingness to go anywhere and do anything for God, regardless of the cost. How did I get to the place that I was so used to living large that I was unwilling to stay within a price range that I could afford?

The houses that I looked at in New Jersey were nice houses, bigger than the house I grew up in as a child, but they were not as nice as the house I had in Texas. I knew this was an ugly thought. It revealed a terrible attitude. So what did I do? I decided to ignore the prodding concerning that ugly thought. I raised my price range and began looking at larger, nicer, more expensive homes. Amy made the adjustment, and we began to look at houses closer to the level of my home in Texas.

When I went back to Texas, I had to figure out how I was going to pay for the more expensive home that I decided to buy. I went to the bank and got approved for the maximum amount that they would loan me. However, that still wasn't going to be enough to buy the type of house I wanted. Then I talked to my dad about loaning me money to buy the more expensive house. He asked how much I would need, and I told him. He told me clearly that he didn't feel comfortable loaning me the extra money. My plan was that it would come out of my future inheritance. I am one of five children, and I suggested we tell my two brothers and two sisters about the loan so that they would be aware of what we were doing. My dad then offered to give me half of what I was asking and keep it our secret. I said no to that because I didn't want to do anything without my siblings' knowledge. Besides, half the money would still not allow us to get the kind of house that I wanted to buy. Reluctantly, my dad finally agreed to loan me the money, though he clearly didn't feel good about it. I explained things to my brothers and sisters, and they said it was okay.

Between borrowing the maximum amount from the bank and the extra loan from my father, I had come up with a plan that would work. I could now buy the house that I wanted. Though my plan to finance the bigger home in New Jersey was risky, if things went as planned, it would work.

I told Toni about wanting a bigger house and the plan to borrow more money. Her sweet response was, "Honey, I trust you. If you think it is a good idea, then I support your decision."

She trusted me entirely, not only with the financial plan, but also with choosing the house. Toni had told me to pick out the house that I thought was best for our family. She had nothing to do with any of the blunders I was about to make.

Planting a church is a difficult and risky undertaking. The World Trade Center had just collapsed, and the economy of the world was falling apart. I was launching out to plant a church in a community where I had never lived before; I hardly knew anyone. In addition, I came up with a plan to buy a large home that would only work financially if everything went just right. That does not sound like a very wise plan.

Amy, my real estate agent, had taken me to see over 120 homes within a three month period. I was real picky, insistent on finding the right house. Finally I picked out a home, we settled on a price, and we closed on a New Jersey house. I was able to move in with a minimum of furniture. Now I had a place to stay when I traveled to New Jersey.

When I was in Texas, I was meeting with people and churches to raise support for the church plant. While in New Jersey, I was building an apartment for my dad so the house would be ready for my family. I was also meeting with people and getting the church started. We had some meetings at my house for prospective church members. Bobby and Heidi had already moved to New Jersey and were ready to help with the planting of the church.

The house was finally ready, and at the end of May, I packed up the house in Texas. Toni and the kids stayed in Texas with some friends while my son Chris and some friends helped me move all our possessions across the country to our new home.

I am the type of person who likes to finish things so we drove non-stop to New Jersey with all of our belongings. I moved the furniture in and set up the entire home: furniture in the right rooms, pictures on the walls, clothes in the closets. Then we all flew back to Texas.

My son Chris had just finished eighth grade and was

not happy about moving to New Jersey. In light of the great sacrifice of leaving his life in Texas, he asked if he could spend a week at Kanakuk Christian Sports Camp in Missouri. I agreed. After arriving back in Texas, Chris boarded a bus to Kanakuk; Toni, JoJo, Briana, and I loaded up in Toni's mini-van and drove from Texas to our new home. My dad went to spend some time at my brother's home in New Jersey until we were settled in. Toni, Brianna, and JoJo had not seen the house; neither had my father.

When we arrived, I carried Toni over the threshold into our new home. We all loved the house.

That weekend, we officially started our church in the living room of our new home. There were about twenty people at our first gathering.

I had planned that if things went smoothly, we'd be okay financially in this house. But, Toni and my father had been having a tough time getting along for a couple of months before the move. Though we didn't know it at the time, my dad was in the early stages of Alzheimer's. In addition, Toni had changed one of her medications, and was not doing so well. Due to the stress of moving twice, she was beginning to slip back into her illness.

Looking back, I can see this so clearly; but at the time, I was completely unaware of these things. A couple of days after we arrived at the New Jersey home, my dad moved in. Just the idea of the move was tough for my dad, and the actual move proved even tougher. The conflict between Toni and my dad was escalating. After our first church gathering that first weekend, I had to drive to Missouri to pick up Chris from camp. While I was away, things in the Centineo house were about to go terribly wrong. And I would be helpless to do anything about it.

Chapter Twenty-Six

Toni vs. Dad

Shortly after I left for Missouri to pick up Chris, Toni and my dad had a major blow-up. Toni called me as I was driving through Indiana and told me what was taking place between her and my dad. I felt so helpless being hours away from New Jersey. Toni left the house that night with the kids and went to her parent's house in Staten Island. While I was away, my older brother and sister stepped in. When I got back to New Jersey with Chris, they told me they had talked to my dad, and he didn't want to live with us anymore. It had taken me six months to find this house in New Jersey and three additional months to renovate my dad's apartment. Six days after my family arrived in New Jersey, my dad doesn't want to live with us anymore. Then my older brother and sister told me that if he moved out, I was going to have to pay back the money he gave me initially for the home in Texas as well as the additional money that he loaned me for the house in New Jersey.

Things had just gone terribly wrong. My financial situation was dependent upon the money that I had borrowed from my dad to purchase the new home. I was devastated because I knew that there was no way I could pay back my dad and keep the house in New Jersey. I certainly hoped I could work things out with my dad.

At this point, I knew the church plant in New Jersey was over. I wasn't giving up yet, but deep down I knew it was over.

The next morning I was in my bedroom spending time with the Lord. (My hot tub was still in Texas ready to be shipped out. I told them to put a hold on the shipment because I didn't know if I was actually going to need it in New Jersey.) While spending time with the Lord trying to figure what was going on, the Lord spoke to me.

"Joe," he said, "this is all happening because you bought too big a house. That prodding in the car about your ugly thought was from me, and you ignored it."

At that moment I felt relieved because I knew it was true. In ignoring God, I had made a huge mistake. I went downstairs to tell Toni what the Lord had said to me.

Toni was sitting in the kitchen with Heidi. They were talking and crying and praying because of the situation with my dad. I told them what the Lord had showed me— that all of the turmoil was rooted in the fact that I ignored the Lord's prodding and bought too big a house.

Toni immediately came to my defense saying she didn't think the house was too big or that I had done anything wrong. Heidi agreed as well. On that morning in New Jersey, I let the girls overrule God's assessment. But I knew they were wrong.

In Philippians 4:11-13, Paul talks about being content:

I am not saying this because I am in need, for I have learned to be content whatever the circumstances. I know what it is to be in need, and I know what it is to have plenty. I have learned the secret of being content in any and every situation, whether well fed or hungry, whether living in plenty or in want. I can do all this through him who gives me strength.

From his prison cell, the Apostle Paul said that he had learned a secret. It was being content regardless of his situation. Paul had learned this lesson, but apparently, I had not. I wasn't content with the thought of living in a smaller house in New Jersey. But, God intended for me to learn this lesson. After all, I was in the School of Brokenness where one majors in lessons of the heart.

At this point, I realized my only hope of staying in New Jersey was if my dad changed his mind and agreed to stay with us. I was working hard to make this happen, spending time with Toni and my dad trying to patch things up. But, I also was aware that Toni was not happy with the way things were going with my dad. I noticed hints of her illness revisiting her. I really didn't know what to do.

I decided I would travel back to Texas for a couple of days to meet with my advisory board to discuss the recent events. I had set up a board of businessmen and pastors to come alongside me in the planting of the church. I was hoping they could give me some wisdom.

While I was in Texas, Toni and my dad had another blow-up, this one was the worst yet. Again, Toni and the kids went to Staten Island to her parents' home. I was trying to talk Toni through things over the phone, and I was having that helpless feeling once again. She emphatically said, "I am not going back to that house if your dad is there!"

Three years before when my dad had asked if he could live with us, we agreed to have him come. I told my dad that he was welcome to live with us, but to never make me decide between him and Toni or between him and my children, because he would always lose out. And now, Toni and the kids were in Staten Island, and she wasn't coming back until he was gone.

When I got back from Texas, I sat down with my dad and told him he had to leave. His response surprised me.

"This is my house, too, and I'm not leaving."

This was difficult enough, but things were getting worse.

I said, "Dad, you have to leave."

"No," he said. "I'm not leaving."

At this point, my brother and sister got involved and finally, my dad agreed to leave.

Asking my dad to leave the house was one the hardest

things that I had ever done. But, I was forced to choose, and my wife and children had to come first. I was devastated.

I knew that unless God stepped in and performed a miracle, we were going to have to leave New Jersey and move back to Texas. My family had been through so much, moving twice in a span of nine months, and now facing this incredible amount of turmoil. More importantly, Toni wasn't doing well. On top of that, I was trying to reconcile moving back to Texas with the call I had received from God to go back to the New York City area. It didn't make any sense. There were more than a hundred people in Texas who were supporting us financially and in prayer, as well as ten churches who were financially supporting us. I had raised $7,200 in monthly support for this church plant. So many people were behind our church plant. A church in Texas paid for our moving expenses. Could I have gotten this call wrong? When I was crying from Dallas through Arkansas on the drive to New York and sensing God calling me, did I get that wrong? I was so sure that God had called me to the New York City area that if I had gotten that wrong, I could never trust myself to lead for God again. I was so confused. I was seeking God for answers, but I just couldn't make sense of everything that was happening. I was crying out to God for direction. I felt alone.

But then God spoke to me. I sensed Him saying, "Joe,

relax. I know you are having trouble reconciling the call to New York with what appears to be your impending return to Texas. Joe, there are four reasons I sent you to New Jersey. The first reason is we had a year to kill."

I remembered when I asked my previous church for their blessing to plant a church in Texas, and they had said they wanted me to wait one year before planting the church. Well, the year was just about up.

I said, "Yeah, you're right, Lord. We did have a year to kill."

Then He gave me the second reason. "Joe, I wanted to test you to see if you would give up something that you loved in order to follow my will."

I remembered how much I loved Arlington and how I really did not want to go back to the New York City area. God was testing me to see if I would leave the place I loved, to go to the place He was calling me to. I had passed the test. I began to feel much better about things. Then He gave me the third reason.

"Joe, I needed to remove your dad from your household."

I loved my dad very much and really enjoyed having him live with us, but he was having a negative impact on my wife and children. So, for the health of my family, God had to remove him from my household. That made a lot of sense. The Lord gave me the fourth reason: "I needed to get your dad's money out of your pocket."

My dad had given us so much money, and the Lord didn't think I needed it. The Lord was more than able to provide for me, and though all of the financial help my dad gave to me was well-intended, the Lord didn't need my dad's help to provide for me.

Hearing these things from God was truly a game changer. I left that prayer time feeling so much more hopeful. I hadn't missed God's call. And, I wasn't such a bad guy, even if I had spent too much money on the house. The four reasons God gave me for why these things were happening were not as incriminating as I first thought. But God had more to say to me concerning this situation. It would be a few weeks before he gave me the other reasons.

A couple of days after God gave me those four reasons, we made the decision to move back to Texas.

Chapter Twenty-Seven

More Than Four Reasons

As I previously mentioned, three denominations were willing to fund our church plant. The Wesleyan Church offered $107,000 over two years; the Christian and Missionary Alliance offered $104,000 over two years; and the Southern Baptists offered no money. They couldn't fund us financially because the Southern Baptists are not that strong in the Northeast. They just didn't have the funds to help us. But for some reason, I felt the Lord strongly leading me to partner with the Southern Baptists. So that's what I did.

I had been through church planting training with the Southern Baptist of Texas Convention (SBTC), and they had also done an assessment on me. I had scored very high on their assessment, and they were excited to have me as one of their planters. I also had a church planting coach in Texas named Craig who worked with the SBTC. He was the first one I called with the news that we were coming back to Texas. Within a couple of hours of that phone call, Craig was able to get a monthly commitment from the SBTC of over $2,000 per month for three years.

I made another phone call to Pantego Christian Academy, the school my children had attended before the move.

They made special provisions for my three children to go back to the school that they had just left, and they allowed us to rent a house on the school property at a discounted rate. All this occurred within a few hours of our making the decision to return to Texas. I felt like God was confirming the decision to go back to Texas with the SBTC funding, the kids getting back into the school, and a discounted and furnished rental house. Things were really looking up for me.

We had been in New Jersey for about three months now and had started the church. There were about thirty people who were attending our church, and they were excited about what God was going to do. Telling this group of people that we were going back to Texas was difficult for me, but they were understanding and supportive.

We put our house up for sale, leaving most of the furniture in the New Jersey home. We packed up the few things that we needed to live in our rental house in Texas in a U-Haul trailer attached to my Ford Explorer, and we began our drive back to Arlington. JoJo rode with me, and Toni was in her Chrysler mini-van with Chris and Brianna following behind. Though I was disappointed in all that had happened, I was excited to be going back to Texas to plant a church.

We left early in the morning for the long ride to Texas. JoJo was in the front, seat-belted in, and sound asleep.

It was then that the Lord spoke to me again. He spoke very clearly and very differently than I had ever heard Him speak to me before. There was a corrective disciplinary tone to what I was hearing in my heart.

I sensed Him saying, "Joe, there are more than four reasons why you are going back to Texas."

He had my full attention as I continued to drive.

He said, "Remember Me testing you to see if you would give up living in a place you love to go somewhere I called you, even though you hated that place? You **made** me test you to see if you would go because of your constant words that despised my call."

I had put God in the position that He had to test me because I constantly said I would not go back to New York. Second, the Lord said,

When you were unwilling to live in a house that you could afford, I was not pleased!"

I began to tear up. Then He showed me the consequences of my ugly attitude.

He said, "First, because of that ugly attitude, the church in New Jersey died. Second, you failed the people—the thirty people in New Jersey who were part of the church as well as the people and the churches back in Texas who sent you. Third, you failed your father. You put him at risk with the financial pressure he felt when you borrowed that extra money from him. And lastly, you failed Toni and your children by putting them on this merry-go-round of moving back and forth."

After this encounter with God, with JoJo sound asleep in the car, I repented and I wept tears of relief. The relief was because, deep down, I always knew that these things were true.

After about thirty minutes of weeping as I drove down the highway, the Lord brought to my mind the story of David and Bathsheba. David was the King of Israel. While David's army was out to battle, David noticed a beautiful woman named Bathsheba bathing. He called her to the palace and had sexual relations with her. Bathsheba was married to a man named Uriah, one of David's loyal soldiers. Soon afterward, Bathsheba let David know she was pregnant. After unsuccessfully attempting to cover up his sin, David finally decided he had to do away with Uriah. David arranged to have Uriah abandoned while on the front lines of battle. The result was that Uriah was killed in battle. David then married Bathsheba, and she gave birth to their son. David was confronted by the prophet Nathan about this terrible sin. David repented and was forgiven, but as a consequence, David and Bathsheba's son died.

As I reflected on this story, I sensed the Lord saying to me: "Joe, David's sin with Bathsheba caused consequences—their son died. Your sin caused the death of the church in New Jersey."

These were sobering words for me to hear, but they were words that I knew to be true. God continued, I am going to give you another chance. As David had more children, you will have another church."

Now I cried tears of relief because God had finally brought me to the place where the truth was out. Of course, Toni was driving behind me and had no idea of the amazing encounter I had just experienced with God. When we stopped for lunch I wanted so badly to tell Toni what the Lord had shown me, but it just wasn't the right setting. I had to wait until that night when we arrived at the hotel. Once we were in the room, I told her what God had shown me. I told her that all that had happened was my fault. Even though she had given me the benefit of the doubt by supporting me and telling me I didn't do anything wrong, that wasn't quite true. God had lovingly and clearly shown me my sin.

We got the kids together, and I repented before my family members and asked them to forgive me. Each one of them forgave me that night. I felt like a thousand pounds had been lifted from my shoulders. I went to sleep that night at peace.

Little did I know that God was going to make sure that I had learned this lesson well. As I fell asleep, I had no idea of what the events of the next day would bring.

Chapter Twenty-Eight

Blowout in Sulphur Springs

The next morning we were back in our vehicles and on our way to Texas. We thought that with a good day of driving, we could make it to Arlington and not have to stay another night in a hotel. We were making great time. After a full day's drive, we stopped for dinner at a Ruby Tuesday in Arkansas. We ate our dinner and decided that we would push hard and try to make it through Arkansas. We continued our drive and finally hit the Texas border. We were all so excited; we were almost home!

As we passed through Sulfur Springs, about two and one-half hours from Arlington, I felt something strange happen to the car. It pulled to the right, and I could feel the rear driver's side tire explode. When that happened, the trailer seemed to take over. We began to spin around on the highway. Though I am sure that things were happening quickly, for me it seemed to be in slow motion. JoJo was sitting in the seat next to me; I was immediately terrified for his safety. We spun around a couple of times, went off the road, and then began flipping down an embankment. I was grabbing for JoJo and screaming his name. After what seemed like an eternity of spinning and flipping, the vehicle and trailer finally came to a stop. The car was lying on its passenger side, and I was hanging in the air sideways, frantically yelling for JoJo. He finally answered.

"Dad! I'm right here!"

He, too, was hanging sideways, securely seat-belted, safe and sound. While the accident was happening, I was sure that JoJo was going to die. To my amazement, neither he nor I had a scratch. A truck driver arrived at the scene and helped us out of the car. The trailer and the car were mangled and destroyed, but to the truck driver's amazement, we were unharmed. The truck driver had witnessed the accident and assured me that it was nothing short of a miracle that we were alive. Behind our vehicle, Toni, Chris, and Brianna had watched the entire accident. They watched the spinning and the flipping of our vehicle, and they, too, were certain that we were dead.

The police arrived at the scene. Everything in the car and the trailer was destroyed. The officers drove us to a hotel and we got a room. Chris was in shock. It took him three hours to be able to speak. Brianna was shaken, but okay. For Toni, witnessing the accident would prove to be the final straw that would break her emotional back. We didn't know it, but her illness was about to launch its fiercest attack on Toni and our family. For me, I was happy that we survived the accident and that JoJo was okay. I kept hugging him and rejoicing in the fact that he was all right.

The next morning I called the U-Haul company to

report the accident, and they reminded me that I did not take out the insurance on the trailer. I would be financially responsible for it. The trailer was valued at $10,000. The car was totaled, and everything in the trailer was destroyed—but I didn't care. If I had to live in a tent, I would be content. My family was safe. That was all that mattered. Perhaps I had learned the secret of being content, whatever the circumstances.

Though I was in the School of Brokenness, it seemed that my most recent lessons were from the School of Discipline. The discipline I was experiencing was not enjoyable, but it was for my good and would bear fruit in my life. I was reminded of God's Word in Hebrews 12:10-11:

> *Our fathers disciplined us for a little while as they thought best; but God disciplines us for our good, in order that we may share in his holiness. No discipline seems pleasant at the time, but painful. Later on, however, it produces a harvest of righteousness and peace for those who have been trained by it.*

God's rebuke was from the heart of a loving Father who knew I needed a heavenly spanking. I needed to accept and endure the discipline that I was experiencing since God was doing it for my good. Though it was a painful time, I knew there was a harvest of righteousness that would be reaped once the discipline had trained me. I looked forward to the harvest.

God still had more to reveal to me. There was more to tell me, more that He had to help me see. Do you remember me mentioning that I was angry at the way some of my previous churches had operated and at how I had been treated by former churches and pastors? That anger had given birth to a judgmental spirit. It was the source of some of my sinful decisions. Needless to say, it had to be dealt with, and God was planning to do just that. Though I was forgiven, there were more lessons to learn, and more consequences to be experienced.

The worst was yet to come.

The School of Brokenness
Part 2

Chapter Twenty-Nine

A Second Chance

When we woke up in Sulfur Springs the next day, we were thankful to be alive but wondered how we were going to get to Arlington. It was a Saturday, and I called my good friend Jim. He made the drive from Arlington, picked us up, and drove us to Arlington. He invited us to spend a couple of days with his family while the final touches were put on our rental house.

That Saturday afternoon as Toni was napping, Jim pulled me aside and said, "Joe, Toni looks terrible." This whole ordeal had taken a toll on her and Jim was taken back by her appearance.

A couple of days later, we moved into our rental home. The square footage was perhaps eleven hundred square feet, but that was fine with me. We had a roof over our heads, and we were all healthy. Jim and Lisa, friends of ours, located some furniture that we were able to borrow, and we went to pick it up. The only bed that was available for Toni and me was a king-sized bed. The master bedroom in an eleven hundred square foot home does not really allow for a king-sized bed. The good news was that the bed fit in the bedroom. The bad news was there wasn't enough room to walk around it. Though making the bed was a challenge, the bed was so close to the wall that we couldn't fall off, which was great when wrestling with my kids.

Now, I'm not a very big guy, but the shower in the master bathroom was so small that I had to walk in sideways. I had to duck to have the water hit my head. The kitchen was pretty small as well. There wasn't enough room in the cabinets for anything more than the few dishes we had. I built shelves for the food. The nice thing was that our food was always on display for anyone who walked into the kitchen. Living in this small house was just fine by me. My family was healthy; we were back in Texas; and I was getting a second chance to plant a church.

One of the things I felt an urgency to do was to have my hot tub installed. Before we moved to New Jersey, my friend Jim called and asked if I wanted a free-standing hot tub. A friend of his had asked Jim if he knew anyone that needed a hot tub. Jim had immediately thought of me. Of course, I said I would take it, and we put the hot tub in storage. I planned to have the hot tub shipped to New Jersey once we had gotten established in our home. The way things turned out, I was sure glad I didn't have it shipped. So, shortly after moving into the rental house, I had the hot tub installed in my backyard. I was good to go—my family was intact, and I had the means to seek God fervently from my hot tub. I couldn't ask for more.

The Lord began to speak to me again. He directed me

to contact all of the people that I had let down in allowing the church in New Jersey to fail. I was to tell them why the church plant had failed. Not just the four reasons, but all the additional reasons the Lord had showed me on the drive back to Arlington.

I began by calling my dad, my brothers, and my sisters. I told them what God had revealed to me and how I had messed up by buying too big a house. I asked each of them to forgive me, and they did. Then the Lord directed me to call each of the families from our church in New Jersey. They already knew about the four reasons why I was leaving, but I called them and told them the rest of the story. I apologized to them, and they, too, forgave me. Then the Lord directed me to call a meeting of the 120 families from Arlington who were supporting us with prayer and financial support. Many of them came to the meeting. I told them why the church had failed. I asked them to forgive me, and I even offered to return all of the money that had been contributed. No one took me up on the offer, but many of the financial supporters stopped their support. And that was fine.

Then the Lord began to help me deal with my anger towards my former churches and church leaders. I had been really angry with the churches that had let me down, particularly Pantego Bible Church. I had seen churches get so caught up in their building programs that they mishandled finances. Pantego Bible Church ran out of money during their relocation because they built too large a sanctuary. There was no money left to properly finish out the buildings for the children or the youth. I had trusted the leaders to handle the relocation and was so angry about the way things turned out. However, God wasn't concerned about Pantego Bible Church. He was concerned with me and my anger. God helped me to realize that my anger needed to be addressed. Ironically, I was angry at Pantego Bible Church for spending too much money on their building, and I did the same thing by spending too much money on my New Jersey home. My anger and unwillingness to forgive caused me to be vulnerable to make the very same mistake.

Jesus said:

Do not judge, or you too will be judged. For in the same way you judge others you will be judged, and with the measure you use, it will be measured to you.
— Matthew 7:1-2

When we are angry and unwilling to forgive someone, we create a dynamic that could cause us to reproduce in our own lives the same offense that we are angry about in others. I went to the leaders of Pantego Bible Church and apologized for judging them. I forgave them, and I was able to release my anger. That was a good thing for me. In turn, they forgave me. Now…I was ready to start Crossroads of Arlington Church.

First on my agenda was to find a location to meet. My rental house living room would not hold very many people, so I began searching for a place to rent. I went to the elementary school where Toni used to work. Though it was available, it was very expensive. Just months before, the school district had tripled the cost of renting to churches. There was no way that we could afford to rent a school.

The next place I went to was the Dottie Lynn Recreational Center. When I walked into the place, I felt like it would be perfect. It had a large foyer, nice classrooms on the first and second floors, and a large gymnasium. I talked to the administrators, and they said they would be happy to have a church rent their facilities. It would cost three hundred dollars per Sunday to rent the entire building. We could come as early as we wanted, and we would have the whole building to ourselves. The facility was perfect; the price was right; and I decided that this would be our location.

Next on my agenda was to get the word out in Arlington that I was about to start a church. I decided to schedule three vision-casting meetings where interested people could come and hear the vision for this church. Pantego Christian Academy graciously allowed me to use their library at no cost, and we set up meetings on three consecutive Tuesday evenings. In those three meetings, we had about sixty different people attend. Some people came once and decided Crossroads would be their church, and others came to each meeting. After our third meeting, we had about fifty people who agreed to be part of our launch team. We scheduled our first church gathering for Sunday, November 3, 2002.

I decided I would start by teaching from the book of James. I diligently prepared my teaching, not sure if anyone other than our launch team would show up to hear my first sermon. The set-up team arrived early that first Sunday morning, and we put things in order. While we were hooking up our make-shift sound system and setting up chairs, I had a fear that not many people were going to show up. We were scheduled to start at 10:00 a.m. but at 9:55 a.m., there were only about ten people in the building. Half of them were my family. I figured we would start a little late and give people a chance to arrive. I was nervously pacing the foyer at 10:05 a.m. when I looked towards the parking lot and saw a large group of people walking towards the door. What a relief! That first Sunday about 100 people filled our seats. The next week we leveled off to about 75 people, and from that point, our church has continued to grow—slowly, but steadily.

There was something very unique, even profound,

about the start of our church. CrossRoads of Arlington Church began on the heels of the greatest failure of my life. That would play a part in shaping the culture of this new church. People who come to CrossRoads of Arlington often comment that we are very loving and very accepting. We love people and nurture people, even those whose lives are a mess. We have a saying at CrossRoads, we don't shoot our wounded, meaning that when people fail, we rally around them rather than beat them up with guilt. The grace I received from God has helped me to be much more sensitive to other people's failures. After all, I have failed greatly myself. The fact that I planted and was the pastor of CrossRoads is proof that God is a God of second chances. When we experience grace, it makes it easier to extend grace. That is the kind of church we are, and I think that warms the heart of God.

Chapter Thirty

Put Your Arms Around It

The church was started, and so many things were finally behind me, but Toni was not doing well. She had gotten a job as a school nurse at a junior high school in Cedar Hill, about 30 minutes from our home. But she was acting strange, paranoid, and even aggressive at times. Something just wasn't right. She had been seeing her doctor, a well-known Christian psychiatrist, weekly. We were trying to get Toni stabilized. She had been through so much stress, and it seemed she was moving inevitably towards another breakdown. Toni and I lived this struggle out loud before the church, seeing no need to hide it from the congregation. They could sense that Toni wasn't doing well, and they were praying for us.

In mid-December, our house in New Jersey sold. We picked up the rest of our furnishings and moved them to Texas. We placed them in storage and began looking for a house in Arlington. The Lord led us to a wonderful home that we could easily afford, since both Toni and I were working. In the first week of February we moved into our new home. I had the hot tub installed, and we were finally settled. My hope was that having our own place would help to stabilize Toni, and she would start to get better.

However, she continued to get worse. We had weekly prayer meetings for the church on Tuesday evenings at the Rec. Center. After we had settled into our new home, we moved the prayer meeting to my house.

Just before one of our prayer meetings in late February, I noticed that Toni was still in the bedroom. I went in to see why she was still there. She said, "I'm not going to be coming to the prayer meeting tonight. I'm going to stay in my room."

When I asked her why she wanted to stay in her room, she said that she didn't feel up to coming. She was tired and wanted to sleep, even though it was only about 6:30 p.m. I walked out of the room feeling scared and angry.

We had our prayer meeting as scheduled, and afterwards, I vented my fear and anger to Rich, our part-time youth pastor. Though I didn't let Toni know that I was angry or afraid, I sure let Rich know how I was feeling. Rich confronted me, and I realized that my anger stemmed from knowing deep down that this was the beginning of the end for Toni. I intuitively sensed that there were going to be some very difficult days ahead for my family. From that point on, I tried the best I could to contain my anger and fear, not wanting to add to Toni's struggles by letting her know how I felt.

Toni began to miss days of work. She was spending as much time as she could in bed, sleeping. Sleeping was her way of escape. Our trips to the doctor were becoming more frequent. We would drive for an hour to get to his office, and she would cry on the way because she was becoming more and more hopeless about her situation. When we got in to see the doctor, he would spend two or three minutes with us, barely making eye contact. He would write out a few prescriptions and tell us to come back in a week. This experience was quite predictable and became a terrible let down for Toni. In spite of all we were doing, Toni continued to get worse.

Years before, Toni had been diagnosed with Obsessive-Compulsive Disorder (OCD). During times of struggle, a person with this disorder needs to stay busy so that they can occupy their minds and not focus on their obsessions. For this reason, Toni's doctor told me to keep Toni functioning, to keep her busy, and to push her to stay busy so that things wouldn't get worse. That is what I did. I pushed her to go to work, to do chores around the house, to get up and do things. What we didn't know at this time was that Toni did not have OCD. Forcing her to continue functioning was causing her condition to worsen. Without knowing it, we were driving her deeper and deeper into her illness and depression.

Toni's mom once again began traveling back and forth to Texas to help us. I was reliving an episode of my life that I did not want to relive. I would cry out to God from my hot tub, pleading with God not to let this happen again. One night, God spoke to me in response to that request.

He said, "Joe, put your arms around this situation and embrace it. You will find my will going through this, not around it."

It was an incredible word from the Lord. Often we find God's will by going through the trials we face, not by having them removed.

The Greek word for "temptation" and for "testing" or "trial" are the same. So when reading the word temptation, it can also be translated as testing or trial. Look at the words Paul penned for us:

No temptation has seized you except what is common to man. And God is faithful; He will not let you be tempted beyond what you can bear. But when you are tempted, He will also provide a way out so that you can stand up under it.
— I Corinthians 10:13

Paul wanted us to know that the trials we face are common; that is, others before us have faced similar tests. Someone else has been there and gone through that before. But God is faithful, and He will not let us be tested beyond what we can bear. He will never give us more than we can handle. He will also provide a way out or a way of escape so that you can continue standing in the midst of the test or trial. That was what God was saying to me as I prayed in my hot tub.

So, I accepted the situation, and I stopped praying for God to take it away. I set my heart and mind on walking through this challenge and not on having it removed. A couple of weeks after this I came home from work in the afternoon and found Toni in bed. I wondered why she wasn't at work. She told me she had quit her job that morning. She asked me not to be mad, but that she just couldn't do it anymore. I assured her I wasn't mad and that I understood that she was no longer able to keep her job. This medical crisis had now become a financial crisis, as well. It would be difficult to pay our bills without Toni's salary. Amazingly, I was back in the place I was just months before in New Jersey. The main difference was that this time, it was not my fault. I didn't over-borrow to buy a house I couldn't afford. Nonetheless, I had no idea how we would survive financially.

After Toni stopped working, she went downhill, slipping into a deep, dark depression. She hardly ate and was barely functioning. She had pretty much stopped talking. I could see her body shutting down, and she seemed to be slowly dying. We were going to the doctor on a weekly basis now, and after one of our brief visits with him, I pulled him aside and asked him if she was dying. He didn't really have an answer for me, but he said at this point they had done all that was medically possible for Toni. What do you do when your doctor tells you that? I decided not to schedule another appointment. It was at this point that Toni's parents stepped in. They said they were taking Toni back to New York indefinitely. I knew this was best. Though Toni did not want to leave our home and family, we all knew that it was best that she go. Her parents flew to Texas and took Toni back to New York.

I was absolutely beside myself. I was scared, numb, and in great need. I was now a single parent with three kids and a brand new church. I told the church everything. They had seen Toni's decline and knew something like this was inevitable. Like me, they had all seen the pain and agony she was going through as her mind betrayed her. The church didn't blame her, and they didn't blame me. I had always taught them that pastors are real people with real problems. They were seeing this first hand, and they saw no reason to lay any blame on either of us. The church simply stood by us.

While Toni was in New York, church members prayed for us, provided us with meals, helped transport my children to church, and basically helped us in any way they could. Though meals provided for us were great for a while, I didn't want to be dependent on others. After all, I didn't know how long Toni was going to be gone, and I felt that as a family, we had to figure out how to survive this storm.

I called a family meeting and told my kids that we had to come together and figure out how to live our lives until mom got better and came home. The congregation continued praying for us, but we stopped the meals and started to work together as a family. We divided up the chores around the house. I discovered places where already prepared meals could be bought, and I learned how to do laundry. We figured out together how to get things done, and I think it was good for us. We were trusting God to help us survive as a family.

Toni's parents decided to take her to another psychiatrist in Manhattan. This doctor decided to admit Toni to a hospital. When I found out about this step, instead of making me feel hopeful, it made me realize just how helpless I had been to help her. I needed Toni's parents to rescue her. Toni's new doctor suspected that Toni was over-medicated and perhaps had been wrongly diagnosed. Just knowing these things, as well as knowing she was in a hospital and I wasn't there, shook me up. Every night after praying in the hot tub, I would get in bed and Toni was not next to me. I would ask myself, "How have I gotten to this place? How has this happened?" My wife was very sick; I was living as if I were a single parent; and I didn't even know if she was going to survive.

Every night I would put the kids to bed, make their

lunches, and then go in the hot tub to spend time with the Lord. One night after getting out of the hot tub, I felt something come over me that I had never felt before. It felt like I was about to crack emotionally. It felt like I was going to break down. But I couldn't do that, not now. I had to take care of my kids. I began to panic because I felt like I really could lose it. This trial was becoming too much for me. That night, God directed me to Romans 5. I read:

> *And we rejoice in the hope of the glory of God. Not only so but we also rejoice in our sufferings, because we know that suffering produces perseverance, perseverance, character; and character, hope. And hope does not disappoint us, because God has poured out His love into our hearts by the Holy Spirit whom He has give us.*
> – Romans 5:3-5

As I read those verses that night feeling like I was on the verge of breaking down, the words instantly touched and healed my breaking heart. In that moment God stepped in and His Word ministered to me so much that my fearful heart was healed. That experience also helped me to understand the horrors of what Toni was experiencing emotionally. I also learned that God can meet us in our time of need and rescue us with His Word. That is exactly what He did for me. As a testimony to the greatness of our God, I can say that during Toni's time of illness, I never missed a Sunday at church.

Toni was now in Columbia Presbyterian Hospital in Manhattan. Toni had become so depressed that she was almost completely non-verbal. Her doctor, a woman named Susan Turner, called me once a week and talked to me about Toni's history. She knew that Toni's mom and I were the closest to Toni and that we understood how she had gotten to this terrible place. Though we didn't know what to label her illness or how to help her, we could give the doctor great insights into making a proper diagnosis. Dr. Turner would spend forty-five minutes on the phone asking me questions and listening to my answers. That was a far cry from our doctor in Texas who spent two to three minutes talking to us while barely making eye contact.

Toni's new doctor was giving us hope that there was more that could be done for Toni; and that Toni could be made well again. Dr. Turner removed Toni from all of her medications, convinced that Toni was over-medicated. She believed that getting her off the meds would allow her to be more accurately diagnosed. After almost two months in the hospital, Toni was diagnosed with Schizoaffective Disorder, a much more serious diagnosis than OCD. Dr. Turner helped me to understand that by thinking she had OCD and by forcing her to function, we had inadvertently driven her deeper and deeper into depression. But now, with the proper diagnosis and the administration of the proper meds along with fervent prayers of our CrossRoads family, Toni was beginning to snap out of the fog she had been in for so long.

One of the things I learned through Toni's ordeal is that when a person is mentally or emotionally sick, they need a skilled psychiatrist, not necessarily a Christian. Now, when we are speaking about counseling, I highly recommend a Christian counselor because I believe it is important when receiving advice to be talking to someone with a Christian world view. But when it comes to a mental illness and the prescribing of medications, we need a good listener who is also a good chemist. If I needed heart surgery, I would want to go to the best, most skilled, most educated, and most experienced heart doctor that I could find. Being a Christian would not be part of the equation when it comes to opening up my chest and working on my heart. I would want someone who is a good surgeon.

I believe in situations like Toni's that involve a severe mental disorder, it is important to find the best psychiatrist possible, regardless of their spiritual beliefs. Dr. Turner was a skilled psychiatrist, and that is exactly what Toni needed. She took the time to understand Toni's illness, and in so doing, was able to make a proper diagnosis. Dr. Turner helped us to understand the severity of Toni's disorder, properly medicated her, and slowly brought her back to good health. Our Christian psychiatrist in Texas, though a wonderful and godly man, had never taken the time to listen to Toni or me or to study her symptoms. Perhaps that is why she was wrongly diagnosed and over-medicated. And remember, when Toni was at her very worst, he told me there was nothing else medicine could do to help her. Though he was sincere in his assessment, he was wrong. There was more that could be done to help Toni, and I am so glad that her mother and father stepped in and got Toni the help she needed. Perhaps they saved her life.

On one of my trips to New York to visit Toni, Dr. Turner sat me down and helped me to understand that the trigger to Toni's illness is stress. She helped me understand that most people with Toni's disorder don't get married, and certainly don't have children. The fact that Toni married a pastor and had three children shows Toni's incredible strength and ability to rise above her circumstances. It also created a situation that could easily trigger her illness. Toni had over-achieved, and in so doing had created the very scenario that could take her down. Dr. Turner emphasized the importance of managing Toni's stress to keep her from having another breakdown.

After I finished talking with Dr. Turner, God spoke to me. He helped me understand that He gave Toni to me as a gift. But, He also gave her to me so I would take care of her and allow her to over-achieve by being married and experiencing the joy of having and raising children. God showed me that part of my purpose in life was to help Toni to do these wonderful things. I was to take care of Toni. Now I could have complained and said, "God, why did you have to give me someone with all these problems?" You see, when Toni gets sick, it's not easy. But God was showing me that I needed to embrace this situation. When we embrace the situations of our lives, we will find God's greatest purpose and experience fulfillment in our lives. When Toni is not being plagued by her disorder, she is the easiest person in the world to live with. She is a loving and kind person. Toni is one of the most wonderful people in the world. Knowing everything that had taken place, I would marry her again in a split second.

When we embrace the situations of our lives, we will find God's purposes and experience fulfillment. Maybe parents give birth to a child that has a handicap. Instead of saying, "No, not me; I can't handle this," put your arms around the situation and experience God's purpose and you will experience fulfillment in your life. Maybe you're in a marriage that is very difficult. You are asking the question, "Why did I marry this person?" Or, "Why can't my spouse be different?" If we stop complaining and accept the person that we married and accept and embrace their weaknesses, we can find God's purpose for our lives. There are all kinds of difficult things in life that we want to run from, but I believe God wants us to put our arms around those things and embrace them so that we will find His purpose for our lives. That is what He taught me through this situation.

After spending 5 months in New York with her parents, two months of which she was hospitalized, Toni came home. She was a new person. She had a clear mind, was happy and functioning. We were united again as a family. In the days and months after Toni's return, God gave me a greater understanding of how I had been responsible for Toni's most recent breakdown. Being angry at churches and church leaders, buying too big a house, and the rest of the New Jersey drama was the source of the stress that took Toni down. In this recent situation, I was the trigger that caused Toni's illness. Perhaps that explains why when Toni's parents delivered her back to us in Texas, her father pulled me aside and sternly said, "Don't let this happen to her again."

Though Toni never complained about the multiple moves and never blamed me for the stress that caused her illness, God helped me understand that my mistakes had created consequences, not only for myself, but for those around me. When a leader fails, the consequences that he faces can have an effect on those around him. But God's grace was there to forgive. As leaders we need to be very careful how we live our lives.

Chapter Thirty-One

My Turn Now

In the spring of 2008, I was five years into the planting of CrossRoads of Arlington Church, and I was having a blast. I was loving God, loving ministry, loving my family, and loving life. Things were going great. Unfortunately, national and international events were about to change things for me. The economic crisis in our nation and across the world personally affected me. I recall one night in particular when gas was predicted to rise to perhaps $7 a gallon. I remember filling up all my family's cars that night and feeling panicked and extremely stressed. Shortly after that scare, the nation experienced the collapse of the housing market. I had bought investment properties in Las Vegas and Florida, two of the states hit hardest by the collapse. When those investments went bad, it created even more stress and anxiety for me. There were political changes on the horizon in America that also created fear and stress in my life.

That summer, I had planned to travel to Berlin to do ministry with a former minor league baseball player named Darren. We were going to work with Young Life Berlin doing baseball clinics in schools.

The night before the trip, I realized that my passport would expire during the plane ride to Germany. I panicked.

I could not sleep much that night. At 6:00 a.m. I began calling the Passport Office in Houston. Around 8:00 a.m. I finally got to talk to someone. I was told that there was no possible way to mail a new passport in time for my flight, and it would not be possible for me to get on the plane with an expiring passport. Since it was just Darren and I going on the trip, if I couldn't go, the mission trip would have to be canceled.

I thought about how many people I was letting down, and I felt horrible. I was letting down my church that had paid for the flight; I was letting down Frank, the Young-Life Berlin Director who had planned this mission trip; I was letting down Darren, who was so excited about going to Germany; and I was letting down God. As I prayed about this, I realized that the only hope I had was to drive to Houston and get my new passport, and then somehow get back to Dallas for my 7:00 p.m. flight.

I worked out a plan to drive to Houston (a 5-hour trip) with a friend named Steve. Hopefully, I would get my new passport, fly from Houston to Dallas, and meet Darren who would have my luggage at the DFW airport in time for my flight.

Steve did the driving and seemed to be going 90 mph, weaving in and out of traffic. I sat in the passenger seat of Steve's car, fighting an overwhelming mood of helplessness and stress. It seemed too much for me to bear.

We got to the Passport Office in Houston and I dashed inside. Within an hour I was back in the car with my renewed passport. Steve drove me straight to the airport in Houston where I was able to book a flight to DFW. The flight was scheduled to land at DFW two hours before my scheduled flight to Germany. Finally, I began to relax and my overwhelming stress began to subside.

When I arrived at the gate in Houston, I learned that the flight to Dallas was being delayed by an hour and a half. Needless to say, the stress was back. Eventually, I boarded the plane and arrived at the DFW gate 30 minutes before the flight to Germany departed. Darren was waiting for me, luggage in hand.

Later, we were able to laugh about it all. We flew to Germany, had a great mission trip, and came home. However, I had no idea how the stress was affecting me.

In September of that year, I had planned to visit a church planter friend in Staten Island and to speak at his church. I had also planned to visit my father while in the New York area. He was living in Upstate New York at a home for Alzheimer's patients. I hadn't seen my dad for about a year and a half. When my sister Chris and I arrived at the facility where he lived, I was quite taken back by his condition. His Alzheimer's was very advanced. I was disturbed by what I saw as I visited with him. My dad had been taken captive by a horrible disease. I began to feel anxious, and then a sense of hopelessness came over me. We visited with my dad for a few hours. We took him to lunch and on walks, but I couldn't wait to leave. Chris dropped me off at the Staten Island Ferry where I planned to take public transportation back to the church planter's home in Staten Island.

As I walked to the ferry, I noticed five tough-looking guys walking behind me. I was born and raised in New York City; situations like this had never scared me before. Again, I had a strange feeling of anxiety when the tough-looking guys walked past me. I put all of these things aside and attributed it to having a bad reaction to discovering my dad's situation.

Two days later, just before flying back to Texas, I learned some very disturbing information about someone who was very close and dear to me. Once again, I felt that all-too-familiar feeling of anxiety and stress churning within me. I couldn't wait to get back to Texas to see Toni and my kids. I would be relieved when this trip was over. Monday evening, I arrived in Texas, happy to be home.

I had a crazy week ahead of me. I had accepted an invitation to speak at Pantego Bible Church's Men's Retreat in Tyler, Texas, that next weekend. When I got to work on Tuesday, I had to prepare three sermons for the men's retreat. Also, I had a wedding on the Saturday afternoon of the retreat. I would have to drive from Tyler to Arlington (a two and a half hour trip) for the wedding, and then drive back to Tyler to finish the retreat on Saturday night. Then, I had to drive back to Arlington to preach at our two Sunday morning services at Crossroads. When I agreed to do all these things, I knew it would be a busy weekend; but as I prepared that week, I knew that I had taken on more than I should have.

I completed my preparations and left the office early Thursday evening. The plan was to leave for the retreat at mid-day on Friday.

When I woke up Friday morning, I felt very, very strange. I was anxious, fearful, and my stomach was twisting. Although all my preparations were done, I felt overwhelmed by the tasks before me. As I traveled to the retreat, my knees were shaking and my stomach was still twisted. I didn't understand what I was feeling.

I struggled to deliver the messages at the retreat on Friday night and Saturday morning, but even though I felt horrible, the messages went great. Perhaps it was a rush of adrenaline that allowed me to preach well. Or, perhaps it was God's anointing?

After the morning session, I drove to my home in Arlington, showered, put on my suit, and drove to the wedding. When I finished officiating at the wedding, I changed clothes and met up with one of my assistant pastors, Gene-O, and we began our drive back to Tyler. In

Dallas, we hit heavy traffic, and it seemed that we might not make it to Tyler in time for the evening meeting. Then we got lost. Feelings of anxiety and stress were stronger than ever. I didn't understand what was happening to me. We made it to Tyler just in the nick of time, and surprisingly, I preached one of the best sermons of my life.

Gene-O dropped me off at my home at one o'clock that morning. I got into the hot tub to pray, and then went to bed. I preached two sermons the following morning at CrossRoads, and then I crashed. All the events of the previous 5 months had culminated in a breakdown.

Chapter Thirty-Two

Anxiety, an Old Friend

As I look back on my life, I can clearly see a pattern of anxiety. When I was ten, I got a newspaper route. It was my first job. The day before I started delivering papers, they gave me a little green book with all the addresses of the houses where I was to deliver newspapers. No one had ever told me that on one side of the street were the odd numbers, and on the other side were the even numbers of homes. I did a practice run to become familiar with the houses where I was to deliver papers. I couldn't figure out where the houses were. I went home and began to have feelings of anxiety. I couldn't sleep. I was freaking out, crying, and experiencing incredible anxiety. My dad went with me the first morning, helped me deliver the newspapers, and I quit the job that afternoon. That was the first of many times that anxiety would get the best of me.

I also remember having sleepless nights totally worried about how I would get my four siblings and my mother and father out of the house if it caught fire. The most stressful thoughts revolved around how I would get my youngest sister, Lori, out of our three-story home. I would stay up at night and worry and worry and worry about this. I never told anyone about it.

When I was about sixteen and in 10th grade, I was a running back on my high school football team. It seemed that when I did well, our team won; and when I didn't do well, our team lost. I began to have fears on the nights before football games that my poor performance would cause my team to lose. This anxiety continued through my senior year. The night before a game, I would not sleep a wink, experiencing intense anxiety and fear of failing on the football field.

At 18 years old, my father bought a landscaping business for me and my older brother. We were new in the business and really didn't know what we were doing when it came to taking care of people's lawns. Most of the other landscaper's lawns were a lush green by late April. In our second year, it was mid-May and our lawns were not looking very good. I began to stress that we were going to lose our customers and our business. I went into a frenzy of fear and anxiety. I drove my brother crazy.

All of these examples of fear can easily be attributed to being obsessive-compulsive or to just being a little anxious and fearful. These things came and passed. They were really no big deal. None of these situations were debilitating, and they were never accompanied by depression. But, when I was twenty-two years old, I had an episode that was different. I began to have some questions about the meaning of life. I was making lots of money in my landscaping business; I was living with the girl I planned to marry, but it seemed to me that there had to be more to life. As I contemplated the meaning of life, I had no answers. I started to work myself into a panic as I feared a meaningless existence. I also began to fear death. As a twenty-two-year-old young man with seemingly everything going for me, anxiety had begun to dominate me. I soon found myself in a serious bout with depression. I never labeled it "depression," but I was miserable. I felt lost and hopeless. This lasted for months. It was during this time that I discovered that the girl I was with had been unfaithful to me. At that point, the bottom completely fell out. In this crisis, I found Jesus Christ as my Savior. Christ rescued me from anxiety and depression and gave me a new life.

When I came to Christ, I realized that I didn't have a meaningless existence, and I didn't need to fear death. It began a long run of incredible joy, peace, and the absence of anxiety. Christ had become my rock. He had become my strength, and He had become the One who anchored my life. Trusting Jesus became the remedy for anxiety and fear. When I had anxious or fearful thoughts, I put my trust in Christ and His Word, and the fear would subside. Christ transformed me from a fearful person into a courageous person.

As a Christian, I did not have a context for what I was about to experience and was completely caught off guard.

Chapter Thirty-Three

Suffering and Sorrow
as Companions

I have had periodic struggles with anxiety my entire life, but in 2008, and the months and years that followed, I came to the realization that I struggle with anxiety, and anxiety can often lead to depression. It has been difficult for me to admit this.

In bringing me to this realization, God has helped me discover a new reality in my life that often involves sorrow and suffering. As I accept this new reality of sorrow and suffering in my life, I find that I can discover His will for my life in an even greater way because God can take sorrow and suffering and transform them into joy and peace.

Perhaps you are thinking, "Joe, didn't Christ come to give life and to give it more abundantly? What's all this talk about sorrow and suffering?"

Christ does give life more abundantly, but I think I am in good company when I talk about having sorrow and suffering as companions in my life. I would like to remind you of a passage of scripture from Isaiah 53 that speaks prophetically about Jesus.

He was despised and rejected by men, a man of sorrows,
and familiar with suffering. Like one from whom men
hide their faces He was despised, and we esteemed Him
not.
– Isaiah 53:3-4

Jesus was called a man of sorrows, familiar with suffering.

Also, in II Corinthians, Paul describes some of the emotions he experienced as he took the Gospel to the world.

Praise be to the God and Father of our Lord Jesus Christ,
the Father of compassion and the God of all comfort,
who comforts us in all our troubles, so that we can com-
fort those in any trouble with the comfort we ourselves
receive from God. For just as the sufferings of Christ
flow over into our lives, so also through Christ our com-
fort overflows. If we are distressed, it is for your comfort
and salvation; if we are comforted, it is for your comfort,
which produces in you patient endurance of the same suf-
ferings we suffer. And our hope for you is firm, because
we know that just as you share in our sufferings, so also
you share in our comfort. We do not want you to be un-
informed, brothers, about the troubles we experienced in
the province of Asia. We were under great pressure, far
beyond our ability to endure, so that we despaired of life.

Indeed, we felt we had received the sentence of death.
But this happened that we might not rely on ourselves
but on God, who raises the dead.

– II Corinthians 1:3-9

Paul talks about sharing in the sufferings of Christ. He talks about being distressed. He talks about being under great pressure (or stress), and despairing of life itself (depression). And of course, Paul learned that Christ would use these things for the sake of others and would, indeed, carry Paul through these emotions. Seeing the place sorrow and suffering played in Jesus' and in Paul's life makes me feel that I am in good company when I experience these things.

Fear and anxiety slowly took a grip on my life and my heart to the point that I could not shake them. I felt like I was in a dark tunnel and there was no way out. I tried to hold it together and continued to pastor the church, hoping my anxiety would pass. This continued for over a month. Finally, on the first Sunday in November on our church's 7th anniversary, I shared my struggles with the congregation, and later, in a meeting with the Elders. I took two weeks off and began the slow journey of coming back from my emotional crash—my meltdown—my breakdown.

During that two-week period, I met with doctors; I

met with other pastors; I read books. Still, I didn't fully understand what was going on. As I tried to make sense of what I was experiencing, I began to realize that I wasn't alone. I discovered that it is very common for pastors to go through this kind of crash. God slowly, but surely, brought me back to health, although now I have a vulnerability to this kind of breakdown. Since the fall of 2008, anxiety shows up unannounced in my life and sometimes leads to times of depression. I am learning to live with this new reality, even as I write these words.

My crash helped me to become much more sensitive to those who suffer emotionally and mentally. When I interact with people who suffer in this way, I know it is so important that I not give simple answers and make unreasonable demands of those who are in the middle of a dark place. It is not helpful to simplify things by telling people, "read the Bible and pray, and you'll feel better." Reading the Bible and praying are wonderful things to do, but saying that to a person gripped by emotional pain might not be helpful. My own personal crash has made me a much better husband, father, and pastor because I can now empathize with people in a greater way than ever before.

Chapter Thirty-Four

Living a Healthy and Balanced Life

My personal encounter with anxiety and depression resulted in my learning ways to prevent and even overcome these emotional attacks. Though this list is not exhaustive, I believe it will prove to be helpful in maintaining good mental health.

Sleep

For about 15 years I had averaged about 6 hours of sleep per night. I did not sleep enough. Lack of sleep can make us more susceptible to anxiety and depression. Even though my lack of sleep was mostly because I was doing something spiritual (I was usually in my hot tub praying), it still put me at risk. I believe that God wants us to take care of our bodies, and that involves eating right and getting enough sleep. I sleep at least 7-8 hours every night.

Exercise

In the early days of my crash, I often felt like I was in a dark tunnel. I was overwhelmed with fear and depression. Someone suggested that I run when I was feeling that way.

After going on a two or three mile run, I noticed the depression often lifted. Cardio exercise causes our bodies to release endorphins that make us feel happy. I learned that exercise is an important part of my emotional well being, so I do a cardio workout 4 times a week.

Medication

There is a stigma in the church concerning medication for depression and anxiety. While taking medication for blood pressure and cholesterol is accepted in the church, taking medication for anxiety and depression is not readily accepted. I am thankful for the medical advances that help us understand the way our minds and emotions function. I encourage you to consider medication for emotional issues, under a doctor's care, of course. I have taken medication for my anxiety and depression.

Biblical Thinking

In the scriptures we are told to control our thoughts, meaning we are to control our brains. Paul tells us to renew our minds and to bring our thoughts captive to the obedience of Christ. When I understood that there is a difference between my mind and my brain, it helped me to realize that I am not a victim of my brain. The control center of the human being is the heart or the soul or the mind. The brain is simply an organ that needs to be controlled and to be trained. Rather than listening to my brain, I need to control my brain. Rather than being the hostage of my brain, I need to allow my heart/soul/mind to determine how my brain operates. I have learned to "bring my thoughts captive to the obedience of Christ" (II Corinthians 10:5).

Boundaries

As a pastor, I had pushed too hard for too long. I kept pushing myself and pushing myself, and I finally broke. I had to come to the place of realizing that there is only one Savior, and His name is Jesus, not Joe. I needed to make sure I was taking care of myself, and that meant occasionally saying "no" to the never-ending requests that come to pastors. I learned the importance of having healthy boundaries for my ministry.

Prayer

Anxiety and depression visit my life unannounced. It is in these times that I find I pray the most. I have learned that God is my comfort, and prayer has become a central part of my life and ministry. I pray more now than I ever had before.

Warfare

We have an enemy who loves to take advantage of our weaknesses and our vulnerabilities. Satan wants nothing more than to destroy us. Though he is a great foe, he can be resisted. He can also be overcome through the name and power of Jesus Christ. I am aware of the attacks of the enemy and do warfare prayer to overcome the attacks of the evil one.

Sovereignty

When we believe in the sovereignty of God, it is so much easier to accept the trials and weaknesses in our lives. Often times we say, "God, why is this happening to me?" This flies in the face of God's sovereignty. When we understand the sovereignty of God, we accept the trials that come our way knowing that God is going to use these trials to accomplish His will for our lives. We can accept our weaknesses knowing that in those weaknesses He will be made strong. I accept and embrace the trials that God allows in my life as well as my own personal weaknesses.

Others

I have learned the importance of having significant

others in our lives. For me, that is my wife Toni who has lovingly walked with me through all of the trials of my life. It also involves some great friends that listen to me, accept me, and love me regardless of what I am facing. I have a group of significant others in my life.

Persevering

If we continue to do the things God calls us to do regardless of how we feel and regardless of what we are going through, we will never stray very far off the path, in spite of what we are "feeling." When we shut down during times of difficulty and darkness, we will find ourselves spiraling downward. I am committed to persevere in time of trouble.

Transparency

Writing this book is perhaps the most transparent thing I have ever done. The Lord has made it very clear to me that I am to share my personal struggles publicly. It is my attempt to help you know that you are not alone in your struggles. While I don't recommend that you share your personal issues in public just yet, I do recommend that you share your struggles with safe people you trust. We can be there for each other and God can use us to help each other. I gladly and joyfully live a transparent life.

In II Corinthians 12, we discover that Paul had a thorn in his flesh, a messenger of Satan to torment him. Though we are not sure exactly what this was, we are sure that Paul wanted it to be removed from his life. Three times Paul pleaded with the Lord to take it away from him, to take this thorn out of his life. God's answer to Paul was "No." God told Paul that His grace would be sufficient because God's power is made perfect in weakness. Some of us have asked God to take away a thorn in our own lives. Perhaps God's answer to us is the same as His answer to Paul. Perhaps God wants you and me to know that His grace is sufficient for us, and His power is made perfect in our weakness. Can you trust that God will use all things in your life to make you more like Jesus?

That is where I stand today. I hope you can have the type of trust that believes that...

...in all things God works for the good of those who love Him, who have been called according to His purpose.
— Romans 8:28

Conclusion

I have now come to the end of my story, though not the end of my journey. I know that there are more lessons for me to learn and my hope and prayer is that I will continue to walk faithfully with my Lord, no matter what comes my way. I want to keep learning and keep growing in my faith until the day that God calls me home.

Your life is also a unique journey, and God wants to take the journey with you. Life has its ups and downs, its good times and its challenging times. God wants to be with you for the entirety of your life journey. Your relationship with God starts when you confess your sin and acknowledge Jesus Christ as your Lord and Savior. Once you take that step, you become a child of God, a follower of Jesus Christ. If you have never trusted Christ as your personal Savior, why not take a few minutes and consider asking Jesus to forgive your sins and come into your life?

I invite you to pray the following prayer:

God, I come before you recognizing that I am a sinner. God, I believe that You sent Your Son Jesus Christ for me. He lived a sinless and perfect life; He died for my sins; and He rose from the dead. Through His death and resurrection, I believe forgiveness is available. I want to receive that forgiveness that comes through faith in Jesus Christ. Jesus, come into my life, forgive my sin, and become my Savior and Lord. I want You to lead and direct my life.

For those of you who have already trusted Christ as Savior, why not pray this prayer:

Lord, I invite You to be a part of my life journey. Help me to seek You with all my heart. I pray that I would have significant encounters with you in the days and years ahead. I pray I would learn to recognize Your voice, and that You would guide and direct me throughout my life journey. I pray this in Jesus name, Amen.

I pray that you will encounter God personally and feel His presence with you. To spend a lifetime in close relationship with God, enjoying the tenderness of His love, listening for His voice impressed upon our hearts, and trusting Him whatever the cost, brings the greatest fulfillment.

God's grace and peace be with you.

Postscript

I hope you have been encouraged by the words and events in this book. I originally shared my journey with the congregation of the church I pastor in a 9-week sermon series. It was so well-received by the church members that several encouraged me to put the series in written form. I polled the congregation to gauge their response. They were in unanimous agreement that my journey should be available in book form. So, in a sense, this book is a gift from CrossRoads of Arlington Church and me to you.

My desire for the sermon series and the book is for people to know that God wants to rescue all people, and He will do so every time,when we call out to Him. Secondly, I want people to know that although salvation secures our eternal destiny, it only begins the lifelong process of being conformed to the image of Jesus Christ. God has many things to teach us. God takes the time to mold each of His children into the person He wants each of us to be. Thirdly, I want followers of Jesus to know that it is possible to have "encounters" with God. When invited, He will invade our lives and give us the guidance and direction we all want and so desperately need.

Though this book has concluded, my life with God continues. I expect that there will be future "encounters with God." Perhaps I will catalogue them, and when it seems the right time, I will share them in a sermon series, and perhaps another book. Until then, let's continue to seek both Him and "Encounters with God" that can change our lives.

Joe

About the Author

Joe Centineo has spent the past 30 years in ministry. He was a Youth Pastor for 17 years in NYC, San Diego, and Arlington, TX. In 2002, Joe founded CrossRoads of Arlington Church and is presently the Lead Pastor. He makes his home in Arlington, Texas. He enjoys working out, watching sports, and landscaping. Joe is married to Toni, and has 3 children: Christopher, Brianna, and JoJo.

www.crossroadsofarlington.org

To order this book, go to:

www.encounterswithgodthebook.com

Missions have become a large part of my life and ministry, and I have partnered with Mission of Hope Haiti to help sponsor children at their school in Titanyen, Haiti. I encourage you to support this worthy ministry with me.

Joe

MISSION OF
HOPE FOR A NATION

The children attend school, using a Christ-centered curriculum. Each child also receives a hot, nutritious meal during the day that he may not have otherwise.

Child sponsorship is a blessing to the student and to you as a sponsor. Sponsors receive regular updates on the child's grades, letters from the student, and are able to send letters of support, as well.

"TODAY we need your help! We need YOU so that we can say yes to 2500 new students! If you have never sponsored a child, this is the time to be a part of what God is doing to change a nation, one child at a time. If each of us would say "YES!" to just one child, every one of these families who has said they want life change for their son or daughter would be able to see that happen this year. Please join me in saying "YES!" today!"

To sponsor a child, and help Mission of Hope affect change in these children's lives, simply go to www.MOHHaiti.org and click on "Child Sponsorship."

Your sponsorship will help provide hope to a child who may otherwise never have an opportunity to receive the gospel of Christ, as well as a quality education.

Brad Johnson,
President
Mission of Hope Haiti

www.MOHHaiti.org